50 Literacy Strategies for Beginning Teachers, 1–8

Third Edition

D0025871

TERRY L. NORTON

Winthrop University, Professor Emeritus

BETTY LOU JACKSON LAND

Winthrop University, Professor Emeritus

Boston   Columbus   Indianapolis   New York   San Francisco   Upper Saddle River
Amsterdam   Cape Town   Dubai   London   Madrid   Milan   Munich   Paris   Montreal   Toronto
Delhi   Mexico City   Sao Paulo   Sydney   Hong Kong   Seoul   Singapore   Taipei   Tokyo

Vice President/Editor-in-Chief: Aurora Martínez Ramos
Editorial Assistant: Michelle Hochberg
Associate Sponsoring Editor: Barbara Strickland
Executive Marketing Manager: Krista Clark
Marketing Manager: Danae April
Production Editor: Karen Mason
Project Manager: Susan Hannahs
Cover Designer: Karen Salzbach
Cover Art: Photodisc/Getty Images Royalty Free
Full-Service Project Management: Sudip Sinha, Aptara®, Inc.
Composition: Aptara®, Inc.
Text Printer/Bindery: Edwards Brothers
Cover Printer: Lehigh-Phoenix Color
Text Font: 10/12 Times

Credits and acknowledgments borrowed from other sources and reproduced, with permission, in this textbook appear on the appropriate page within the text.

Library of Congress Cataloging-in-Publication Data
Norton, Terry.
  50 literacy strategies for beginning teachers, 1–8/Terry L. Norton,
Betty Lou Jackson Land. —3rd ed.
    p. cm.
  Includes bibliographical references and web resources.
  ISBN-13: 978-0-13-269006-5
  ISBN-10: 0-13-269006-3
  1. Language arts (Elementary)   2. Language arts (Middle school)
3. First year teachers. I. Land, Betty Lou Jackson. II. Title.
III. Title: Fifty literacy strategies for beginning teachers, 1–8.
  LB1576.N845 2012
  372.6'044—dc22
                           2011008199

10 9 8 7 6 5 4 3 2 1

www.pearsonhighered.com

ISBN-10:   0-13-269006-3
ISBN-13: 978-0-13-269006-5

Contents

Preface

Welcome to the third edition of *50 Literacy Strategies for Beginning Teachers, 1–8*. Like the previous editions, this one represents our shared thinking about effective techniques for developing student competence in literacy. Based on our combined experience of almost seventy years as educators in the field of language arts, the third edition maintains our core assumptions about literacy learning and teaching. These assumptions derive from our knowledge of the research base and best practice in literacy instruction and are discussed more completely under Essential Features from Previous Editions. We have found that the application of these beliefs has worked especially well with the diverse students whom we have served in the Learning Improvement Center at Winthrop University, where we taught both preservice and inservice teachers. Here is an overview of the changes in this edition and what we have retained from the two earlier ones.

New to the Third Edition

Along with incorporating suggested changes from our readers and users, we have added the following:

- **An Introduction for Each of the Five Parts on Literacy Strategies**

  Word Recognition

    The introduction explains word recognition or word perception skills—sight words, context clues, structural or morphemic analysis, and phonics.

  Vocabulary

    Because word recognition assists in decoding the pronunciation of words but does not always help in deriving word meanings, the introduction to this section explains the importance of understanding vocabulary concepts, particularly for content area reading.

  Comprehension

    Comprehension is the mastery of an integrated whole in the construction of meaning rather than the isolated use of individual competencies.

  Writing

    The introduction explores the link between writers as good readers and readers as good writers.

  Listening and Speaking

    The introduction to this new section explains the interconnections among all the language arts and gives particular emphasis to providing sheltered instruction to English learners in the development of oral language competence.

- **Four New Strategies for Listening and Speaking**

  Conversational Puppets

    English learners improve conversational English as they retell stories with puppets as scaffolding aids.

  Directed Listening–Thinking Activity with a T-Chart

    English learners increase both conversational and academic English through the use of this strategy with a recommended graphic organizer to help organize thinking.

Echo Reading

This strategy illustrates ways to improve various micro- and macro-components of oral language from sound-symbol relationship to phrasing to sentence fluency as English learners grow in automaticity.

Literary Posters

Using prompts from the teacher and graphic organizers, English learners gain facility with literacy in organizing and presenting ideas.

- **Integration of Several Strategies from the Second Edition to Emphasize Greater Instructional Connections**

The combination of Venn Diagram with Comparison-Contrast Chart, synthesis of Pocket Charts for word recognition and comprehension, and placing together Story Pyramid and Three-Dimensional Text Pyramid more closely integrate variations on teaching strategies.

- **An Appendix with an Annotated List of Websites**
- **An Updated List of Professional References for Further Reading**
- **An Expanded List of Children's Literature Used to Demonstrate Strategies**
- **A Revised Matrix for Ready Reference of Strategies**

Essential Features from Previous Editions

Our Core Assumptions

The following core beliefs undergird the literacy strategies presented in this book:

- students actively seek to construct meaning as they grow in literacy;
- literacy develops over time and includes each of the language arts of reading, writing, listening, speaking, and visually representing, all of which are interrelated and mutually support one another;
- classroom growth in literacy occurs best where language is not fragmented and otherwise used for inauthentic purposes;
- literacy development improves when language is used in functional settings with authentic *literature*— that is, literacy competencies are best fostered through real literature used for real purposes;
- teachers contribute to student acquisition of literacy through direct instruction and scaffolding of learning, which includes activating, building, and maintaining background knowledge in learners and modeling, guided practice, and eventual independent practice as learners take ownership for their accomplishments.

For English learners, scaffolding and the term "sheltered instruction" have much in common. Part VI discusses their similarities and offers suggestions for incorporating these techniques with the strategies described both there and throughout the text.

Organization and Special Features

Lesson plans may follow many formats. This book recommends an instructional framework that divides literacy lessons into three basic parts: what happens *before* students read or are read to, what happens *during* reading, and what happens *after* reading. This book offers ideas to create direct instruction, scaffolding, and sheltered instruction for learners through building, activating, and maintaining background knowledge as preparation for learning, through providing assistance during learning, and through elaboration and application as extensions of learning. Following this instructional framework for a *before, during,* and *after* approach for literacy lessons, teachers will more readily encourage students to be active participants in the construction of meaning.

Our goal has been to write clearly so that anyone involved in the literacy development of students will be able to use the strategies in this book. New and experienced teachers, tutors in clinical settings, paraprofessionals, and interested parents should find the strategies helpful in instructing learners once they have been assessed and need particular interventions to bolster strengths or to overcome needs in literacy. The examples from authentic literature that illustrate each strategy—whether for word recognition, vocabulary development, comprehension, writing, or listening and speaking—serve as instances of how to teach literacy competencies within a meaningful context. We encourage users of this book to seek further ways to adapt the strategies and to use them with the literature in which their students are currently engaged.

As strategies are incorporated into lessons, we suggest that students receive explicit descriptions of *what* the strategy is as an aid to growth in literacy, *why* it is helpful as a technique in developing literacy, *how* the strategy works, and *when* learners can apply it in either a classroom or an independent setting.

Although we could have organized this book in a number of ways, we decided to categorize the strategies according to the literacy competency that each one seems to best develop: word recognition, vocabulary development, comprehension, writing, and listening and speaking. The last two areas concerning oral language are essential to growth in the other areas. Therefore, Part VI, which is new, targets listening and speaking, particularly for students with limited English proficiency, although all learners can benefit from instruction to improve oral language facility.

Because the language arts are interrelated and growth in one enhances growth in the others, many of the strategies will fit into multiple areas, including the newly added strategies targeting English learners. Hence, we have added these to the matrix on the inside front cover to provide a handy guide to show cross connections among various strategies and literacy competencies.

Acknowledgements

We wish to thank the reviewers of our manuscript for their comments and insights: Patricia J. Pollifrone, Gannon University; Kristen H. Turner, Fordham University; and Beth Dykstra Van Meeteren, University of Northern Iowa.

In addition, we want to thank the many gifted preservice and inservice teachers we have taught in courses at Winthrop University. Their implementation of the strategies included in this book has aided us immeasurably in writing it, fine tuning each strategy, and ensuring its usefulness with students. We also wish to thank our former students and graduate assistants Elizabeth Hall Epps, Sara Carey Howard, Jamie Kyzer, and Stephanie Stancil for their technical assistance on many parts of the text. We dedicate this book to the students who will benefit from its use.

Terry L. Norton
Professor Emeritus of Reading Education

Betty Lou Jackson Land
Professor Emeritus of Reading Education

PART I

Creating Successful Literacy Lessons

Format for Literacy Lessons

Effective literacy lessons have a similar underlying structure, no matter what the content of the lesson, whether the subject is dogs and cats or birds and bats. The same holds true for the literacy focus area of the lesson, whether it is deriving the meaning of a word from context or understanding story grammar through story mapping. This underlying structure also applies to lessons on narrative or expository text, no matter what the grade level of learners, whether kindergarten or beyond. The framework upon which a literacy plan is built has three core components that follow a specific instructional sequence of activities that occur *before* reading, *during* reading, and *after* reading.

In the *before*, or prereading, stage the teacher establishes for students a purpose for learning by describing what the topic of the lesson is and why it is important. Concurrent with the discussion of purpose is an activation of schema, or prior knowledge, that learners possess concerning the topic. If the teacher discovers that students have little or no prior knowledge, then background experiences must be established and related to the content of the lesson. Besides activating current background or implanting new knowledge, the prereading stage involves motivating reader interest in the topic. Thus, *before* reading occurs, both cognitive and affective domains of learning are crucial considerations of good literacy instruction that will prepare students for the *during* reading phase of a lesson.

During reading, students interact with text and bring to their learning the schema and interest aroused *before* reading. The teacher's role is to prompt active responses to reading by encouraging students to talk, write, think, or be creative as they construct meaning from text. Much of what students comprehend at this stage of a literacy lesson will derive from the success of the preparatory activities that came *before* reading.

After reading is a follow-up stage. At this point in the instructional framework, the teacher and students extend ideas from the lesson by elaborating further upon them, applying the ideas in different contexts, or making connections to other reading and life experiences. In short, postreading is a time of enrichment for learners.

Along with the aforementioned three-stage instructional framework, effective literacy lessons should be embedded with a universal teaching strategy composed of several steps. These may vary as to whether they occur *before, during,* or *after* reading and as to the particular emphasis allotted to each. Procedures for this generalizable teaching strategy follow.

Procedures for Generalizable Teaching Strategy

The generalizable teaching strategy contained within the instructional framework of literacy lessons has six steps. These should be part of any specific strategy the teacher uses to foster growth in literacy competencies such as word recognition, vocabulary, comprehension, and writing. For example, if the teacher is developing student facility with story grammar elements like setting, characters, problem, problem-resolution attempts, resolution, and theme, a specific strategy that might aid student understanding of these components is a story pyramid or a variation thereon. (See pages 86–90.) As use of the story pyramid unfolds throughout the literacy lesson, we suggest its deployment should be explicitly related to students in terms of the following six steps of the generalizable teaching strategy.

Step 1: Explain WHAT

The teacher should explain *what* a story pyramid is. This would normally occur *before* reading as part of building background, this time for a specific strategy, not just for a specific content.

Step 2: Ask WHY

The teacher should explain *why* a story pyramid is helpful in developing an understanding of story grammar. This step, too, would likely occur *before* reading as part of the motivation for learning.

Step 3: Ask WHEN

As a further part of *before* reading, the teacher should indicate to students *when* to use a story pyramid—that is, when one is trying to understand the organization of narrative text (i.e., stories). Again, this step probably is best suited for *before* reading.

Step 4: MODEL how

At this point, the teacher may also wish to engage in the fourth step of the generalizable teaching strategy—*modeling how* to do a story pyramid with something students have already completed reading, further activating prior knowledge and relating it to new learning. Thus, *modeling how* to complete in part or in whole a story pyramid may be done *before* reading. However, *modeling* might occur *during* or *after* reading as students answer questions and react to the literature they are presently studying.

Step 5: Require GUIDED PRACTICE

When students engage in unfamiliar strategies to achieve growth in literacy, they need guided practice. For instance, in completing a story pyramid for the first time, learners will profit by having the teacher direct their work through positive reinforcement of correct answers and corrective feedback on incorrect or incomplete ones. Guided practice requires the teacher to serve as a mentor, helping students work through interactions with text as they move toward independence in learning. This step may take place *during* or *after* reading in the instructional sequence.

Step 6: Provide opportunities for INDEPENDENT PRACTICE

Independent practice is the final step of the generalizable teaching strategy. In the case of a story pyramid, students complete the pyramid as they map the organization of a narrative selection by themselves. They are on their own in the *after* reading phase of a literacy lesson.

When teachers plan and deliver instruction, they often focus exclusively on steps 1 and 6 of the generalizable teaching strategy. For example, in teaching a literature selection in which they use a specific strategy like a story pyramid, they may tell students what a story pyramid is and then expect them to complete one as part of a postreading check for comprehension. However, short-circuiting instruction in this way may lead to frustration on the part of learners. Steps 2 through 5 are essential components of creating success in literacy development.

The story pyramid is only one of numerous specific literacy strategies available to teachers, many of them described in detail in the different sections of this book. Nonetheless, the procedures given here for the generalizable teaching strategy should be used concurrently with any specific strategy selected for a learner's needs in a literacy lesson. (See Figure I–1.)

Teacher's Name: *Miss Ginger Lark*
Grade Level: *Grade Three*
Literacy Area of Focus: *Story grammar elements including character, setting, problem-resolution, and theme*
Assessment Source: *Informal reading inventory with narrative retelling; teacher observation*
Literature Used: *Arthur's Teacher Trouble,* by Marc Brown

ACTIVITIES	TEACHING PROCEDURES (before, during, and after reading)	TEACHER REFLECTIONS (How did the lesson go?)
Before Reading		
• Introduce purpose statement for students. • Activate prior knowledge or build background knowledge. • Engage learner interest. • Create a story web chart.	• To activate prior knowledge, ask questions: "How did you feel about your teacher on the first day of school? Did you think he or she was mean? What did you think after you were in class for a while? What do teachers do when students do not listen? Would you think a teacher was mean if he got angry with his students for not listening?" • Say: "We will be reading a story about a teacher that everyone thinks is the meanest teacher in school. As we read this story, we will be looking for specific information such as the names of the story characters, where the story takes place, and events that happen in the story. As we learn about this information, we will put it in a chart that organizes the information to help us remember what we have read." • "Let's begin by taking a picture walk through our story, *Arthur's Teacher Trouble,* by Marc Brown. I will point out characters and locations in the story during our picture walk. I would like you to predict what you think will happen when we read the story."	

FIGURE I–1 Example of a Successful Literacy Lesson Plan

ACTIVITIES	TEACHING PROCEDURES (before, during and after reading)	TEACHER REFLECTIONS (How did the lesson go?)
During Reading		
• Engage students in shared reading: reading *aloud,* reading *along,* reading *alone.* • Discuss story elements to complete the story web.	• Ensure all students have a copy of *Arthur's Teacher Trouble.* Then, start by reading the beginning of the book *aloud* including the part that tells about the spelling contest and that introduces Arthur's teacher, Mr. Ratburn. Check to see that students are following along in their books. • After a while, ask students to orally read *along* with you the part of the story that tells about the class studying for the spelling contest. • Then, ask students to finish the book *alone,* reading silently the part of the story that tells about the spelling contest. • During the reading *aloud,* reading *along,* and reading *alone,* stop to ask students to respond to the characters' actions by discussing what Arthur learned or how he changed. Guide the questioning to help students derive an understanding of the theme of the story and the central problem or key conflict.	

FIGURE I–1 *Continued*

ACTIVITIES	TEACHING PROCEDURES (before, during and after reading)	TEACHER REFLECTIONS (How did the lesson go?)
After Reading		
• Model how to complete a story web that includes characters, setting, problem-resolution, and theme. • Engage students in guided practice, prompting them to find the story elements. • Provide independent practice, prompting if needed, to help students complete a new story web for a different story. • Use the story web chart for an extension activity for writing a summary of the original story.	• Introduce the story web chart. (See Figure I–2.) Say: "This is a web that will help you think about different parts of the story. It is shaped like a spider web because parts of the story branch out from the central idea of the story. In this web, you will see that, to help us understand the elements of a story, we need to find the names of the main characters, the story setting, the problem the story tells about, and the solution or resolution for that problem. It will also help us think about the theme or main idea of the story." • Beginning with the bubble for main character, model how to fill in the story web chart. "The name of our story today is *Arthur's Teacher Trouble,* by Marc Brown, so I will write that in the center of the web. Although there were other characters, the main character is Arthur, so I will fill his name in the circle called 'Main Character.' Are there any other names I should put in this circle?" • If needed, complete the whole chart together as a class as a part of the modeling process. If students understand how to complete the chart, provide them with guided practice time to fill it in. Scaffold instruction in order to work with small groups of students who need more direction. • For independent practice, ask students to read a new story and try completing a story web chart for it.	

FIGURE I–1 *Continued*

Purpose: To discuss and summarize story grammar elements of setting, main characters, problem, resolution, and theme.

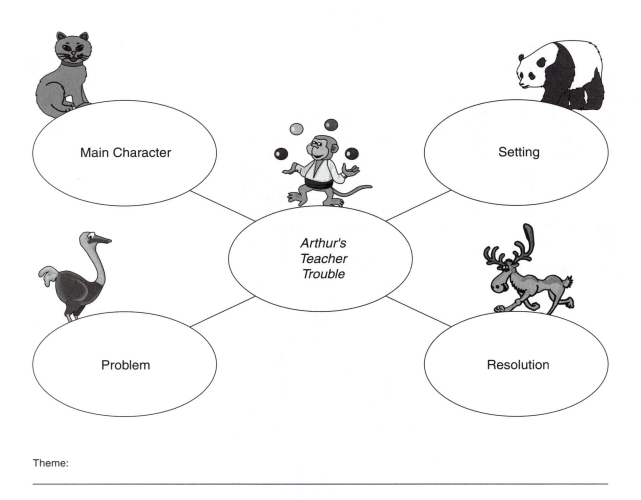

Theme:

_____

_____

Now that we have a story web, you can use it as an outline to write a summary of the story. Your summary must be a brief statement that tells the setting, the main characters, their problem or goal, how they resolve the problem or find the goal, and the theme of the story.

Written Summary of Story:

_____

_____

_____

_____

FIGURE I–2   Story Web Chart

▌Further Reading

Taylor, B., Harris, L. A., Pearson, P. D., & Garcia, G. (1995). *Reading difficulties: Instruction and assessment* (2nd ed.). New York: McGraw-Hill.

Tompkins, G. E. (2005). *Language arts: Patterns of Practice* (6th ed.). Upper Saddle River, NJ: Merrill/Prentice Hall.

Tierney, R. J., & Readence, J. E. (2000). *Reading strategies and practices: A compendium* (5th ed.). Boston: Allyn & Bacon.

PART II

Word Recognition Strategies: Sight Words, Context Clues, Morphemic (Structural) Analysis, Phonic Analysis

In the early grades, word recognition competencies have a significant place in the scope and sequence of reading instruction provided by school district curriculum guides and basal readers, or published sets of leveled texts accompanied by teacher guides and other adjunct materials. Word recognition, sometimes called "word perception," refers to a student's knowing the pronunciation and meaning of a word—that is, being able to figure out an unknown word. This section focuses on pronunciation, whereas Part III, Vocabulary Strategies, concentrates on teaching word meanings. Among word competencies are sight words, phonic analysis, context clues, morphemic or structural analysis, and the use of dictionaries. The last four may be termed "word attack skills" which involve decoding or deriving the pronunciation. Of these, the last three—context clues, morphemic analysis, and the dictionary—may also aid in figuring out the meaning of an unknown word. A quick look at the meanings of word recognition competencies and their implications for teaching will be helpful. We have concentrated on sight words, context clues, morphemic analysis, and phonics, saving it for last because of some special issues regarding this aspect of teaching reading. Because dictionary usage may also be thought of as a study competency as part of applying reference materials, it is not discussed here.

Sight Words

When readers recognize how to pronounce a word and know its meaning, they are using sight words. Mature readers know most words at sight, and this knowing makes reading fast and easy. These words may be those the student has memorized. Sometimes the term "sight words" means the method of teaching until a word becomes automatically recognized or pronounced at sight. However, readers will encounter words not known on sight so that other word recognition competencies are necessary, but automaticity, or the immediate recognition of a word, is the ultimate aim for the learner.

Context Clues

Strategic readers often rely on context clues by using either a picture accompanying print or the text surrounding an unknown word. Sometimes, the target word may be a sight word that has multiple meanings so that the reader has to decide which specific one makes sense within the present context. The word "run," for example, has many meanings as in jogging, candidacy for election, dripping rain water on a window pane, or a tear in one's hosiery. Learners must access context clues to narrow the particular meaning. They also are helpful when the same word has different pronunciations depending upon its meaning. "Bass" may be a fish in one context or a singer with a deep voice in another. "Lead" may be something contained in pencils, or it may be what the head of an organization or a group does.

At other times, a target word may be part of a reader's oral language but presents itself in print for the first time as in the sentence "The astronauts traveled through space to Mars." In this case, a student would need to use context clues to make an inference about the pronunciation of the word "astronauts" that is part of listening and speaking vocabulary but may not be part of the reader's print repertoire.

On yet other occasions, a word may be completely new and not part of the student's ability in listening and speaking as with "apprenticeship" in "He completed his apprenticeship at the local barber shop by watching and imitating skilled and experienced barbers." Even if learners cannot pronounce "apprenticeship," the sentence contains enough context clues for them to derive the word's meaning, although they may need cuing, prompting, and modeling from a teacher.

Pictures may provide aids to meaning when the meaning of a word is inferential or not explicitly stated. In the sentence "It was cool outside, so Rose put on her sweater," the student may not know how to pronounce the word "sweater," but if there is a picture of a girl dressing with a sweater before she leaves her house, the student has a clue as to what the word is.

Students may also need instructional guidance with punctuation marks because these, too, may signal meanings within a specific context. Question marks and exclamation points aid readers with a writer's intended message, and quotation marks assist in determining who a speaker is. Commas may signal pauses to prevent misreading of a sentence.

Context clues are vital if students are to become effective readers, whatever their grade levels. Strategic use of context is crucial as students delve into informational text where the vocabulary load tends to be greater and more difficult than in narrative writing. If a student encounters the following sentence in a social studies text, context clues are essential to infer the meaning of the word "cataract." "High in the mountains, the cataract poured its spray on the explorers as it tumbled toward the valley below in a thunderous roar." If learners must turn to a dictionary or glossary each time they come across sentences like this one, then meaning is impaired as reading becomes a burdensome task and automaticity falters.

Morphemic or Structural Analysis

Readers sometimes may derive the pronunciation and meaning of an unknown word through any morphemes that it contains. Morphemes are structural units of meaning within words. Just as a phoneme is the smallest unit of sound within a language and a grapheme, whether a letter or combination of letters, is the smallest written unit used to represent a sound, so a morpheme is the smallest unit of meaning within a language. Morphemes are of two types, bound and free. A bound morpheme must be attached to another morpheme or other morphemes to form a word, and a free morpheme forms a word by itself. The word "unhappy," for instance, has the prefix "un-" as a bound morpheme and the root or base word "happy" as a free morpheme.

In using morphemic analysis to derive either pronunciation or meaning, the base is first examined—in this case, "happy." Then the prefix "un-" is studied to determine how it alters the meaning so that "unhappy" means "not happy." If "farmer" is the target word, then the base "farm," a place for growing food, is examined to see how it becomes a person when the bound morpheme, or suffix, "-er" is added. Teachers should be cautious in selecting words for morphemic analysis so that they have clearly identifiable structural units of bound and free morphemes. "Restate" is a much better choice than "repeat." The first word has the prefix "re-" that recognizably alters the meaning of the base "state," whereas the second word does not have an identifiable base, at least in English, for the prefix to change its meaning in a way that would make sense to struggling readers. Students can comprehend that "restate" means to "state again" but find little that is understandable when "repeat" is defined as to "peat again."

The study of contractions is also part of morphemic analysis because they are two free morphemes collapsed into one: "cannot" to "can't," "will not" to "won't," "have not" to "haven't," etc. Teachers may present contractions as sight words and later have students analyze their meaning units or separate morphemes. Alternatively, teachers may give students the two words and have students form contractions from them.

Another component of this word recognition competency is compounds composed of two or more free morphemes. Each word in the compound must stand alone and contribute to its meaning. "Jellybean" is a compound because the structural elements of both "jelly," having to do with texture, and "bean," having to do with the shape, may stand alone as independent words and help readers understand the meaning of the two compounded. On the other hand, "carrot" is not a compound because neither "car" nor "rot" contribute to its meaning, although both may be real words. In presenting this aspect of morphemic analysis, teachers will find it necessary to review words carefully to be certain that they are indeed compounds. "Together" would be an incorrect choice to share with students, but "sometimes" would be a correct one.

A technique to avoid is to tell readers to look for little words in big words as in "together" which has "to get her." None of these has anything to do with the meaning of the whole word. In "nation" are the words "at" and "on," but neither is a morpheme contributing to the word's meaning. Instead, teachers should suggest that students look for the chunks of meaning as in the word "unhappiness" where the base "happy," the prefix "un-" and the suffix "-ness" each combine to form a new concept. If students already know "happy" as a sight word, teachers can guide them in analyzing how both the prefix and suffix alter its meaning. Teachers should also call attention to spelling changes in the root word "happy" with "y" becoming "i" in the new word when the suffix "-ness" is added.

Phonic Analysis

Much debate among reading specialists concerns the word attack or decoding competency of phonic analysis. Some people mistakenly think that it is the *only* way to decipher words. Teachers should be careful with this belief because many words cannot be sounded out based on their letters and letter combinations. "Come," "was," "what" are among a few such instances.

The strategies suggested in this book encourage teachers to use a beginning sound or sounds of a known sight word along with context clues or word associations to figure out an unknown target word. For example, if students encounter in their reading the word "book" and it is not part of their stock of sight words, teachers should encourage them to think of words already known like "baby" or "look." By using the initial /b/ sound from "baby" and the letter combinations "-ook" in "look," the reader can figure out the pronunciation of "book." Mature readers engage in a similar process of analytic phonics when they encounter unknown words by applying what they know to the unknown. Often, this type of instruction is part of spelling, a topic beyond the scope of the discussion in this book. Although phonics is a useful and valuable word attack skill, instruction in this competency should probably be completed by around third grade where a shift to spelling is desirable.

A few notes of caution are in order in teaching sound-symbol relationships. Although English is an alphabetic language, it has more sounds than the twenty-six letters of its alphabet. One sound or phoneme in English may be represented by one letter or by a combination of letters. Also, one letter may represent several sounds. The letter combination "sh" in "ship" represents the same sound as the "t" in "education" or the "s" in "sugar." These letters or letter combinations are graphemes or written symbols to signify a single sound in the language. Another complication is illustrated by the consonant "c." As a grapheme, it may symbolize the sound /k/ as in "can" or the sound /s/ as in "city." Even more problematic are vowels in English. Vowel graphemes, whether one letter or a combination of letters, serve to represent a wide variety of phonemes. The letter "o" may stand for a long sound as in "go" or a short sound as in "hot." When doubled, the combination or vowel grapheme may yet again sound different in "look" and "moon," and when by itself in "to" or "horn," the grapheme takes on further separate sounds.

As a result of the way English may express sound-symbol relationships, readers may encounter difficulties. Learners who have a hearing impairment, who do not have an auditory learning style, or who speak regional or local dialects may find reading programs problematic that rely heavily on phonics. If a student reads aloud the word "creek" and calls it "crick," teachers should allow for this dialect difference in pronunciation.

Interaction of Word Recognition Competencies During Reading

When previewing text that they will be assigning or using in the classroom, teachers should notice words that will likely be new for their students and decide which word recognition competencies to present to their learners as part of a *before, during,* and *after* lesson framework. Phonics may not be the best choice for scaffolding and sheltered instruction as teachers seek ways to provide the necessary help for success in reading. Other word recognition competencies or a combination of several may be more strategic. Interactions between readers and the teacher in informal observations that occur during daily lessons often provide insights into how students apply word recognition to decode unknown words. The sentence "Jim likes cherry ice cream" will be used to illustrate some of the ways that students often apply one or a combination of word recognition competencies and how sometimes this application is not the most strategic for the target word.

If a student immediately reads "Jim likes cherry ice cream," the teacher may assume that all of the words are more than likely sight words because they have been pronounced automatically without hesitation. If a student sees the word "cherry," does not know its pronunciation, and then looks at a picture showing a carton of cherry ice cream and correctly pronounces the word, then the reader is using a form of context clues because the illustration has provided a hint. The learner's strategic reading has paid off in this instance.

In another example, if a student cannot pronounce "cherry" but thinks "I know the word 'chop,' how to say my friend's name 'Jerry,'" and then uses the beginning sound /ch/ of the first word and adds the ending "-erry" of the second word to form "cherry," the reader has engaged in analytic phonics. The learner has derived the pronunciation of the unknown word based on known words that are part of background knowledge and is again reading strategically. However, if a student pronounces the target word "cherry" as "chocolate," the teacher can logically infer that the reader has some knowledge of phonics because of the correct pronunciation of the beginning sound /ch/ but does not know the rime or phonogram "-erry." Perhaps some direct instruction concerning these kinds of spelling patterns would help the learner become a more strategic reader.

As a final example with the word "likes," if a student figures it out by first saying "like" and then adding the sound of the bound morpheme or suffix "-s," then the teacher has evidence that this reader knows something about morphemic or structural analysis as an aid to pronunciation. Another inference might be that the student pronounced the word based on knowledge of the sight word "like" and the sound of /s/ as a phoneme or unit of sound. In any event, the teacher may conclude that the learner is successfully using strategies to attack the target word.

As is evident from this discussion, students often combine skills interactively in more or less efficient ways in the act of reading. Sometime, word recognition competencies occur so instantaneously that the teacher cannot detect which ones readers are using. As long as students comprehend the meaning of the words and are not just pronouncing them without understanding, such automaticity is an indicator that the material is easy to read.

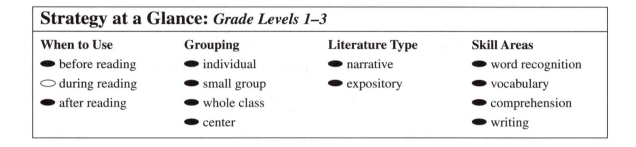

1

Pocket Chart

EL Beneficial when working with English learners

Strategy at a Glance: *Grade Levels 1–3*			
When to Use	**Grouping**	**Literature Type**	**Skill Areas**
● before reading	● individual	● narrative	● word recognition
○ during reading	● small group	● expository	● vocabulary
● after reading	● whole class		● comprehension
	● center		● writing

Purpose

To develop the ability to construct meaning after a story has been read and to increase sight vocabulary for pronouncing words automatically for reading fluency

Literature Used

Free Fall, by David Wiesner
Just Me and My Dad, by Mercer Mayer

When to Use

Before and after reading

Description of Strategy

Pocket charts are large, heavy paper, cloth, or plastic charts that have pockets where words or sentences may be placed. Teachers may prefer to make their own pocket chart using a poster board with clothespins attached. (See Figure 1–1.) Words from a story or poem may be printed on strips or on word cards of the same size. A teacher might also use sentences from student dictation and create individual word cards of the words in each sentence. The teacher can then use the word cards from the selected literature for a number of different activities.

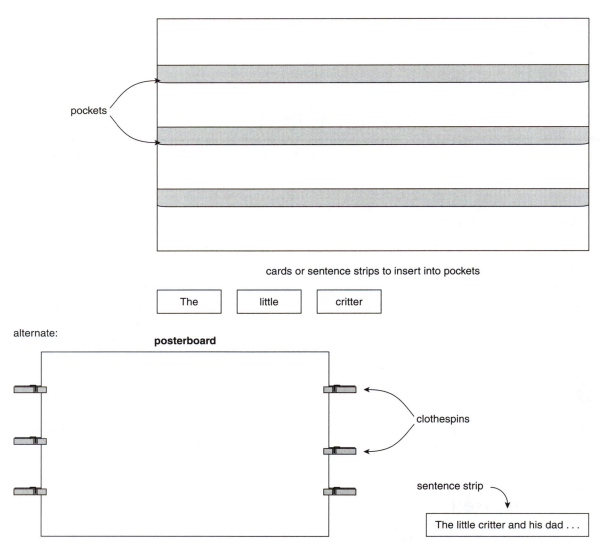

cards or sentence strips to insert into pockets

| The | little | critter |

alternate:

posterboard

The reader attaches sentences in order to the posterboard using the clothespins.

FIGURE 1–1   Pocket Chart

Procedures for Use

1. Because a wordless picture book was chosen for this strategy, students will create a story to go with the illustrations. The teacher and students will first interact with the book and each other through discussion and questioning about the storyline revealed through the pictures. The teacher then records the students' partial or full retelling of the story one sentence at a time on sentence strips. It will be helpful as reinforcement of sight words for learners to watch as the teacher records and recites their rendition. The length of the story will depend on the students and the book. Less able learners may tell a story about only one picture from a wordless book, while those who are more capable may create a narrative for all of the illustrations. Retellings of longer texts may need to occur over several lessons.

2. The teacher reads the story retelling *aloud*; then the teacher and students orally read the story *along* together; and finally the students read the story *aloud* and *alone*. (This technique is referred to as read *aloud, along, alone.*)

The boy is dreaming.

He goes places in his dream.

3. The teacher now uses the sentence strips and writes each word of the retold story on a separate card. The cards should be the same size and written in the style of letters students are accustomed to reading. They should watch the teacher record the words and should pronounce them with the teacher.

The		boy		is		dreaming.

4. The teacher puts the words to the story in the pocket chart in order.

5. The teacher once again reads the retelling *aloud*; teacher and students then read the story *along together orally*; and finally students read the story *aloud* and *alone* as the teacher sweeps his or her fingers under the words on the pocket chart to help readers with the flow. These repetitions will enhance the students' ability to read the story fluently.

6. The teacher now takes out two to three word cards that the students could not read from the pocket chart and places them on a table. The teacher also may get out a box of sand in which these students will write the word from the word card. (This method will reinforce these words as sight words for tactile learners.) The students write each word with a finger in the sand as the word is slowly pronounced, a procedure that should be repeated for all word cards on the table that were removed from the pocket chart and that students could not read. It is best to select only a few (two to three) difficult words at a time for such sight word practice. The visual image, or configuration, of the words selected should be different.

7. As an additional reinforcement activity, the teacher may next place all of the word cards from the pocket chart story on the table in a shuffled stack. From these, students place the word cards in the correct order in the pocket chart so that both the teacher and students can again read the story *aloud* in the correct sequence. (See the alternate idea below.)

8. Students may read the story *aloud* and *alone* if further practice and reinforcement are needed.

Alternate Idea

Pocket charts are helpful in scaffolding sequence as part of reading comprehension. The teacher follows the first two procedures as given above for recording sentence strips and exposes students to the sentences through a read *aloud*, *along*, *alone* format similar to that described in steps three, fours, and five. Because the focus is on the sequence of story details, the teacher will not cut apart the strips into individual words but leave the sentences intact. The strips are now arranged out of order so that readers must place them in the sequence in which the story took place. Use of pocket charts in this way allows students to physically manipulate events in the plot as they learn about this aspect of story grammar. As with individual word cards discussed in step three above, the sentence strips should be of equal length so that a variation in size will not act as an extraneous decoding clue for readers.

For less-able learners, the teacher may scaffold the activity by asking questions to help students recall the sequence of events. Possible questions and responses for this kind of sheltered instruction for *Just Me and My Dad* are:

Question: Where were the little critter and his dad at the beginning of the story?

Response: The little critter and his dad were at home.

Question: Where did the little critter and his dad go next?

Response: They went to a campsite.

Question: Once they found a suitable campsite, what did the little critter and his dad do?

Response: They went to the river to fish.

Question: After they finished fishing, what did the two do next?

Response: They went back to their campsite.

During these prompts, the teacher may want to engage in purposeful rereading of relevant parts of the book so that students listen again in order to formulate answers. If students have their own copies of the text, the teacher may direct them to reread certain passages to determine the correct event for a question.

1. After the teacher has written the events on sentence strips, these can be randomly ordered for students to place in correct sequence on the pocket chart. The teacher should make sure that students can read the strips to ascertain adequate sight word recognition and to determine the need for further instruction.

2. To develop competency in visual interpretation, students may wish to add an illustration to each sentence strip event of the story.

Further Reading

Cooper, J. D. (2000). *Literacy: Helping children construct meaning* (4th ed.). Boston: Houghton Mifflin.

Gunning, T. (2005). *Creating literacy instruction for all students* (5th ed.). Boston: Allyn & Bacon.

Reutzel, D. R., & Cooter, R. (2000). *Teaching children to read: Putting the pieces together* (3rd ed.). Columbus, OH: Merrill.

Word Wall for Sound-Symbol Relationships

EL Beneficial when working with English learners

Strategy at a Glance: *Grade Levels 1–3*			
When to Use	**Grouping**	**Literature Type**	**Skill Areas**
○ before reading	○ individual	● narrative	● word recognition
○ during reading	● small group	● expository	● vocabulary
● after reading	● whole class		○ comprehension
	○ center		○ writing

Purpose

To integrate writing and reading and to reinforce grapheme-phoneme (sound-symbol) relationships

Literature Used

The Dog That Called the Signals, by Matt Christopher

Teammates, by Peter Golenbock

When to Use

After reading

Description of Strategy

A word wall is an instructional tool that may build on the need to further develop word recognition skills. It may be used with students who need assistance with beginning or ending consonant sounds and medial long or short vowel sounds. The words may come from a book, topic of interest, or words the teacher knows that learners are having difficulty with. The words are placed on a poster or chart (i.e., the word wall) for students to see and refer to in further reading and writing activities. The words on the wall should follow a language pattern as with the initial consonant /f/ for *The Dog That Called the Signals* or with the short medial /a/ sound illustrated in *Teammates*.

Procedures for Use

1. With students, the teacher selects a book containing words that they need to work on and that have the same pattern, in this case the initial sound of /f/ in words in *The Dog That Called the Signals* or the short medial /a/ in *Teammates*.

2. With the teacher's assistance, students choose from the book words that follow the identified sound pattern, in this case /f/ or short /a/. A chart, picture, diagram, web, and so on may be used by the teacher as a place to write the words and hang them on the wall. (See examples for *The Dog That Called the Signals* and *Teammates* in Figures 2–1 and 2–2.) These should be written in the style that learners will encounter in print. The words may be written on cards and displayed on the word wall with tape, tacks, or Velcro. This way, the words are easily moved around for a variety of purposes.

3. For additional practice, the teacher works with students to select other words to illustrate the sound pattern. This activity will help students solidify their knowledge of the pattern as they make connections to their experiential background with words already familiar to them and not in their reading.

4. As the teacher does other kinds of literacy activities in the class, he or she may choose words from the word wall to use in lessons and in examples. These may include writing activities. For example, an extension of this strategy would be to take the words from the word wall and write a sentence using each one or to write a summary of the book or a whole story incorporating some or all of the words.

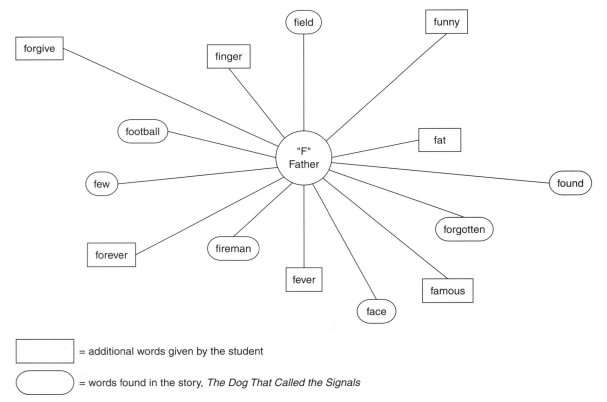

□ = additional words given by the student

◯ = words found in the story, *The Dog That Called the Signals*

FIGURE 2–1   Example for Initial Consonant /f/ in *The Dog Called the Signals*
Note: Words that begin with a blend, such as "flower" and "friend," should not be used to illustrate initial /f/ when students are first learning the sound.

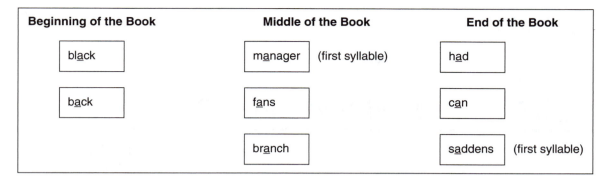

FIGURE 2–2   Example for Medial Short /a/ in *Teammates*

Further Reading

Cunningham, P. (2000). *Phonics they use* (3rd ed.). New York: Longman.

Cunningham, P., & Allington, R. (1994). *Classrooms that work.* New York: HarperCollins.

Cunningham, P. M., Moore, S. A., Cunningham, J. W., & Moore, D. W. (1995). *Reading and writing in elementary classrooms: Strategies and observations* (3rd ed.). White Plains, NY: Longman.

Gunning, T. (2005). *Creating literacy instruction for all students* (5th ed.). Boston: Allyn & Bacon.

Johns, J., & Lenski, S. D. (2001). *Improving reading: Strategies and resources* (3rd ed.). Dubuque, IA: Kendall/Hunt.

Reutzel, D. R., & Cooter, R. (2000). *Teaching children to read: Putting the pieces together* (3rd ed.). Columbus, OH: Merrill.

Tompkins, G. E. (2005). *Language arts: Patterns of practice* (6th ed.). Upper Saddle River, NJ: Merrill/Prentice Hall.

Vacca, J. A. L., Vacca, R. T., & Gove, M. K. (2000). *Reading and learning to read* (4th ed.). New York: Addison Wesley Longman.

Modified Cloze Technique

EL   Beneficial when working with English learners

When to Use	Grouping	Literature Type	Skill Areas
○ before reading	● individual	● narrative	● word recognition
● during reading	● small group	● expository	● vocabulary
● after reading	● whole class		● comprehension
	○ center		○ writing

Purpose

To develop the ability to use context clues and grapheme-phoneme awareness (sound-symbol relationships) for pronunciation of words and construction of meaning

Literature Used

"The Man in the Moon As He Sails the Sky," an anonymous poem

When to Use

During or after reading

Description of Strategy

Cloze is an instructional tool that uses a blank space to show the deletion of words or word parts, such as letters, and that can readily be adapted to satisfy the needs of struggling readers. For those who need assistance with beginning, middle, or ending sounds (graphophonemic clues), a letter or letters may be provided as a prompt at the beginning, middle, or end of a blank. Students must then use additional clues (contextual) to determine what the missing word is. Because this strategy is a modified cloze approach, it is not necessary to have a fixed deletion pattern of every *n*th word, as is often the case when cloze is used for prereading assessment. The teacher simply deletes words with the beginning, middle, or ending sound that students need practice with, as in the example in step 4 of the following procedures. The blanks, however, should be of equal length so as not to provide extraneous typographical clues. Because the modified cloze technique requires learners to use context clues, it also works well as a vocabulary development strategy for deriving word meaning.

Procedures for Use

1. The teacher selects a poem or story that has an interesting pattern and opportunities for using context clues to help pronounce words and construct meaning.

2. After the poem is selected, it is retyped in large print, and letter from the stimulus words are omitted, such as those containing medial short /i/ in the consonant-vowel-consonant pattern (CVC) in the poem, "The Man in the Moon As He Sails the Sky." (See lines 2–8 of the poem.)

3. Before students supply the missing words, they and the teacher discuss how to figure out what the missing words are. The teacher may model the process, or do a "think aloud," with one example and then encourage learners to reflect on the use of the surrounding words to determine the missing word for each of the other blanks.

4. The following poem builds both grapheme-phoneme awareness (in this case with short medial /i/) and contextual awareness. However, in this poem, the initial /m/ sound could be emphasized, if needed, in words like "Man," "Moon," "made," "mistake," "milk," and "milky," so that lines might read as "The M_____ in the M_____ as he sails the sky. . . ." Poetry is good to use because of the repetition of sounds with either assonance (for vowels) or alliteration (for consonants).

> The Man in the Moon as he sails the sky
> Is a very remarkable sk____pper,
> But he made a m____stake when he tried to take
> A drink of m____lk from the d____pper.
> He d____pped right out of the M____lky Way
> And slowly and carefully f____lled it.
> The B____g Bear growled and the L___ttle Bear howled,
> And frightened h____m so that he sp____lled it!

5. For further practice, students might discuss words like "is," "in," and "it" in the poem because these, too, illustrate short /i/ at the beginning of words.

Further Reading

Cunningham, P. (2000). *Phonics they use* (3rd ed.). New York: Longman.

Cunningham, P., & Allington, R. (1994). *Classrooms that work*. New York: HarperCollins.

Graves, M., Juel, C., & Graves, B. (1998). *Teaching reading in the 21st century*. Needham Heights, MA: Allyn & Bacon.

Harris, A. J., & Sipay, E. R. (1990). *How to increase reading ability: A guide to developmental and remedial methods* (9th ed.). New York: Longman.

Johns, J., & Lenski, S. D. (2001). *Improving reading: Strategies and resources* (3rd ed.). Dubuque, IA: Kendall/Hunt.

Reutzel, D. R., & Cooter, R. (2000). *Teaching children to read: Putting the pieces together* (3rd ed.). Columbus, OH: Merrill.

Tierney, R. J., & Readence, J. E. (2000). *Reading strategies and practices: A compendium* (5th ed.). Boston: Allyn & Bacon.

Masking

EL Beneficial when working with English learners

Strategy at a Glance: *Grade Levels 1–3*

When to Use	Grouping	Literature Type	Skill Areas
○ before reading	● individual	● narrative	● word recognition
○ during reading	● small group	● expository	● vocabulary
● after reading	○ whole class		○ comprehension
	○ center		○ writing

Purpose

To help students develop grapheme-phoneme (sound-symbol) awareness by focusing on word beginnings and endings that are familiar to them

Literature Used

The Blah, by Jack Kent

When to Use

After reading

Description of Strategy

Masking may be used to allow learners to focus on a single word sound, or a grapheme-phoneme component, in familiar sight words to extend automaticity to unknown words. Students will learn that by simply changing the initial or final letter(s), they can form new words. The technique, as described here, is thus helpful in improving the word recognition skill of phonics, which is most successful when students first develop a concept of a word and then relate it to the printed letters for sounds. Accordingly, the teacher should read the book first so that the students are able to hear each of the words used in context. The teacher should switch the initial and final phonemes—that is, whichever sounds are chosen for emphasis—of selected words to form new words.

Procedures for Use

1. The literature selected for this masking exercise is *The Blah*. It contains words with spelling patterns for rhyming words to develop sound-symbol relationships.

2. After the literature has been read in a shared mode such as *along* or *aloud*, the teacher selects several words the students know—for example, "sad" and "fish."

3. The first words selected should be words where the initial phoneme can be changed to make new words. Changing the initial phoneme develops rhyming words (that is, word families based on phonograms like –ad in "sad" or –ish in "fish"). It is easier for students to hear the beginning sound of the word rather than the final sound.

4. Masking slides and holders should be made prior to the activity. The teacher creates a masking slide by first deciding on the phonogram to be taught. The teacher can have every possible letter option for the phonogram written on the card for the masking activity or leave a couple of examples blank and let the students provide letters that could be substituted to form new words.

5. The following illustration is for "fish," a word from *The Blah*. The masking strip shows how a rhyming word family is created with "wish," "dish," and "swish." Of course, combinations of letters such as consonant blends and digraphs, as with "sw" for "swish," may be used instead of single letters to create the rhyming word family.

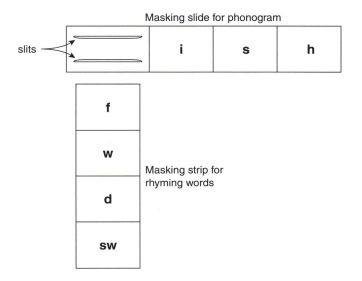

6. When students are able to use successfully the masking activity with initial letters or letter combinations, the teacher can begin working with masking activities to change the final sounds of words as in the following masking slide and strip:

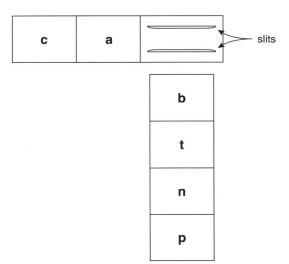

Further Reading

Cunningham, P. (2000). *Phonics they use* (3rd ed.). New York: Longman.

Cunningham, P., & Allington, R. (1994). *Classrooms that work*. New York: HarperCollins.

Graves, M., Juel, C., & Graves, B. (1998). *Teaching reading in the 21st century*. Needham Heights, MA: Allyn & Bacon.

Johns, J., & Lenski, S. D. (2001). *Improving reading: Strategies and resources* (3rd ed.). Dubuque, IA: Kendall/Hunt.

Reutzel, D. R., & Cooter, R. (2000). *Teaching children to read: Putting the pieces together* (3rd ed.). Columbus, OH: Merrill.

5 Language Experience Approach for Sight Word Development

EL   Beneficial when working with English learners

Strategy at a Glance: *Grade Levels All*			
When to Use	**Grouping**	**Literature Type**	**Skill Areas**
● before reading	● individual	● narrative	● word recognition
● during reading	● small group	● expository	● vocabulary
● after reading	● whole class		● comprehension
	○ center		● writing

Purpose

To improve reading by helping students develop a basic sight word vocabulary for automaticity

Literature Used

The Rainbow Fish, by Marcus Pfister

When to Use

Before, during, and after reading

Description of Strategy

In the language experience approach, students, individually or in groups, dictate a story as the teacher records it. The written story is based on the students' oral language and personal experience, whether built by the teacher or already possessed by the students. These features of language experience increase the likelihood that students, particularly low-achieving readers, will be able to read and comprehend the dictated text because the words are their own and not those of another writer, which may or may not correspond to the students' language. Student success with this approach provides a motivational boost for learners because they usually take pride in the experience stories created. Older, less able readers will often find that the stories are at an appropriate maturity level, unlike stories in beginning basals, which may be at an appropriate reading ability level but seem too immature in content. Although the language experience approach may be used to teach many aspects of literacy, such as sequencing, spelling, comprehension of expository or narrative grammar of texts, and so forth, the focus in the following procedures is on using language experience stories to develop a stock of basic sight words to promote automaticity in reading.

The teacher selects any topic important to the students. This serves as the basis for the dictated experience. Such a topic might be "my favorite place to visit," "my summer vacation," or "my favorite animal." If used for a group story, the experience might be about the class pet, a field trip, or another experience with which the class is familiar. In addition, literature can be used to build background and write a story summary. The literature might be a story in a basal reader, a passage from a content area textbook like science, or a children's book like *The Rainbow Fish.*

Procedures for Use

1. The teacher engages the student or group in a brief discussion about *The Rainbow Fish* in order to build background. A picture walk would be an appropriate strategy to incorporate at this stage. (See pages 91–92.)

2. The teacher reads the book *aloud.* During this step, guided listening questions that call for prediction or that help learners attend to significant concepts and details such as important vocabulary words or key elements of story grammar like setting, characters, sequence of events, and descriptive passages may help improve comprehension and later retelling.

3. Students may orally summarize the story or part of the story as the teacher records what is dictated. (In some instances, the dictation may be about an experience that is merely related to the literature or that is inspired by it, as in the following example in item 8 on *The Rainbow Fish.*) Whether chart paper, the chalkboard, or notebook paper is used to record the dictation, students should be able to see the words as the teacher reads them *aloud* in order to aid in establishing them as sight words. The teacher should be sure the words are those of the students themselves so that they feel ownership for the story. It is important to keep the dictation short at first. If the story is too long, less capable learners may not be able to read it.

4. When the dictation is completed, the teacher should read the dictated story *aloud* and point to each word as students follow *along.* This procedure further helps to build a sight word vocabulary for words that students already possess as part of a speaking vocabulary but have not yet learned in their written form. As the teacher reads the story, learners should be given an opportunity to make any changes.

5. Once changes are completed, the teacher and students read the story together, with the teacher again pointing with smooth motion at each word as it is read *along.*

6. Students now try reading the story *alone.* If there are any words at this point that they cannot pronounce, the teacher should note these for later practice and review. These might go into a personal word bank or word wall that may serve as individual dictionaries for future reference for reading or for writing stories.

7. When the teacher feels confident that students have mastered the words as sight words for the dictated story, a final activity could be to have the story rewritten as an additional summary and illustrated with a picture if students so desire.

8. Figure 5–1 shows an experience story, titled "The Colorful Fish," based on *The Rainbow Fish.* The words in the list are those with which further practice was needed by the children who dictated the story.

The Colorful Fish

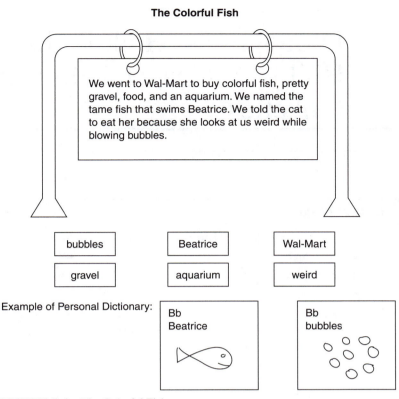

We went to Wal-Mart to buy colorful fish, pretty gravel, food, and an aquarium. We named the tame fish that swims Beatrice. We told the cat to eat her because she looks at us weird while blowing bubbles.

bubbles	Beatrice	Wal-Mart
gravel	aquarium	weird

Example of Personal Dictionary:

Bb
Beatrice

Bb
bubbles

FIGURE 5–1   The Colorful Fish

Further Reading

Cunningham, P. (2000). *Phonics they use* (3rd ed.). New York: Longman.

Cunningham, P., & Allington, R. (1994). *Classrooms that work.* New York: HarperCollins.

Cunningham, P. M., Moore, S. A., Cunningham, J. W., & Moore, D. W. (1995). *Reading and writing in elementary classrooms: Strategies and observations* (3rd ed.). White Plains, NY: Longman.

Graves, M., Juel, C., & Graves, B. (1998). *Teaching reading in the 21st century.* Needham Heights, MA: Allyn & Bacon.

Gunning, T. (2005). *Creating literacy instruction for all students* (5th ed.). Boston: Allyn & Bacon.

Norton, D. E., & Norton, S. E. (2003). *Through the eyes of a child: An introduction to children's literature* (6th ed.). Upper Saddle River, NJ: Merrill/Prentice Hall.

Reutzel, D. R., & Cooter, R. (2000). *Teaching children to read: Putting the pieces together* (3rd ed.). Columbus, OH: Merrill.

Taylor, B., Harris, L. A., Pearson, P. D., & Garcia, G. (1995). *Reading difficulties: Instruction and assessment* (2nd ed.). New York: McGraw-Hill.

Tierney, R. J., & Readence, J. E. (2000). *Reading strategies and practices: A compendium* (5th ed.). Boston: Allyn & Bacon.

Tompkins, G. E. (2005). *Language arts: Patterns of practice* (6th ed.). Upper Saddle River, NJ: Merrill/Prentice Hall.

6 Phonograms: Hink Pinks, Hinky Pinkies, and Hinkety Pinketies

Strategy at a Glance: *Grade Levels All*

When to Use	Grouping	Literature Type	Skill Areas
○ before reading	● individual	● narrative	● word recognition
○ during reading	● small group	● expository	● vocabulary
● after reading	● whole class		○ comprehension
	○ center		● writing

Purpose

To reinforce word patterns or graphemic bases and develop spelling ability

Literature Used

Fish Is Fish, by Leo Lionni

When to Use

After reading

Description of Strategy

Hink pinks, hinky pinkies, or hinkety pinketies are pairs of rhyming words that are answers to riddles. The teacher gives the riddle, and the students respond with a pair of rhyming words.

Procedures for Use

1. *Before* reading, the teacher introduces the book *Fish Is Fish* to students by showing the cover and beginning a discussion about their experiences with fish. (A pet? A fishing trip to the river? Fish in tanks at the pet store?)

2. The teacher encourages students to listen to the story about two friends. One friend is a fish and one is a frog. The teacher explains that, after the story, she will ask the class to think of words that sound alike at the end such as "frog," "log," and "dog," or "fish," "wish," and "dish." The teacher reads the story while the class listens.

3. *During* reading, the teacher briefly pauses several times to get the students to orally name a word that rhymes with a word from the story. Examples may be "<u>weeds</u>" and "seeds"; "<u>bank</u>" and "tank"; "<u>jump</u>" and "bump." The underlined words are in the story.

4. *After* reading, the teacher explains that she is going to give some clues and the class will have to think of rhyming words to guess the riddle. For example, in the first clue below, "a dream or request made by a water animal," the answer would be a "fish wish." The rhyming words connect in their meaning to create a new word phrase. Some ideas are listed. (Underlined words are from the story.)

Clue	Hink Pinks
a dream or request made by a water animal from our story	<u>fish</u> - wish
an animal that is in the air, so it does not get wet	<u>dry</u> - butterfly
a big stick in the water with an animal on it trying to get warm	<u>frog</u> - log
water you can swim in that is not hot	<u>cool</u> - pool
a place to play—except at night	<u>dark</u> - park
a special time on the first date after the month of April	<u>May</u> - day

5. For those learners having difficulty guessing the answers to the riddles, the teacher can provide one of the words in the hink pink and the students can guess the rhyming word. "A <u>frog</u> sits on a big stick to get dry. This would be a <u>frog</u>-_____ ."

6. The teacher could begin with the riddles in this way to provide scaffolding. Gradually, she would give the clues as written and let the class guess both rhyming words. Eventually, boys and girls can create their own riddles with rhyming words as answers.

7. Pairs of words that are two-syllable answers to riddles are called hinky pinkies, while answers of three syllables are called hinkety pinketies.

Examples:

Hinky Pinkies	**Hinkety Pinketies**
a violent tale	stealing by thieves who think they are better than other people
<u>gory</u> - story	<u>robbery</u> - snobbery

Further Reading

Gipe, J. P. (2006). *Multiple paths to literacy: Assessment and differentiated instruction for diverse learners, K–12* (6th ed.). Upper Saddle River, NJ: Merrill/Prentice Hall.

Tompkins, G. E. (2005). *Language arts: Patterns of practice* (6th ed.). Upper Saddle River, NJ: Merrill/Prentice Hall.

7

Word Building

Strategy at a Glance: *Grade Levels 1–2*			
When to Use	**Grouping**	**Literature Type**	**Skill Areas**
○ before reading	● individual	● narrative	● word recognition
○ during reading	● small group	● expository	○ vocabulary
● after reading	● whole class		○ comprehension
	○ center		○ writing

Purpose

To develop phonemic awareness or sound-symbol (phoneme-grapheme) correspondence and spelling

Literature Use

How to Talk to Your Dog, by Jean Craighead George

When to Use

After reading

Description of Strategy

A teacher selects key words from books that the students are reading and that exemplify particular phonic concepts or spelling patterns. Each student is given a set of individual alphabet letters. These may be written on cards or may be plastic letters. A sheet is provided to each student and has boxes on it representing the number of phonemes contained in each word. If a word has three phonemes, such as /dog/, three boxes are on the page, and the students are given no more than six letters to choose from. The teacher leads the students to "build" or spell a variety of words by "pushing" the letters or letter combinations into the appropriate sound box.

Procedures for Use

1. The teacher orally reads *How to Talk to Your Dog*.

2. After reading, the teacher explains that the students are going to use letters to build some words that are in the book. The teacher identifies words for study.

3. Each student has a sheet with three boxes drawn on it. Each student also has three alphabet letters that are the same size or smaller than the boxes. In this example, the word "dog" is selected. (See Figure 7–1.)

4. On an overhead projector, chart paper, or board, the teacher models how to listen to the sounds in the word "dog" by dragging out the voice as "dog" is pronounced. The teacher explains that three sounds are heard. The teacher might say, "I am looking for three letters that represent those sounds so that I can build or spell this word."

5. Slowly, the teacher slides a **d** into the first box. The students follow the lead. The same process occurs with the **o** and **g**. The teacher observes to be sure that each student has built the word correctly. The teacher and class then say the word slowly together as they track under the word with their fingers. Then the students say the word fast as they underline the word with their fingers.

6. The students remove the letters from the boxes, mix them up, and see whether they can "build" the word independently.

7. The teacher instructs the class to add a letter to the ones on the desk, so that each learner now has four letters—a **d**, **o**, **g**, and any other letter. In Figure 7–2 the letter **m** is added. It is best to select a letter that is configured differently from the ones in the word "dog." For example, **p**, **q**, or **b** would be poor choices because they look similar to **d** or **g**. After these letters are mixed up, the students see whether they can still spell "dog" with the extraneous letter **m** not being used.

8. Depending on the level of the class, the teacher may advance the activity to initial consonant substitutions, then to final consonant substitutions, then to vowel substitutions. (See the example that follows in Figure 7–3 where **t** replaces **g** at the end of the word to form "dot.")

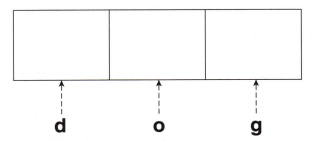

FIGURE 7–1   Example of Word Building Boxes with *How to Talk to Your Dog*

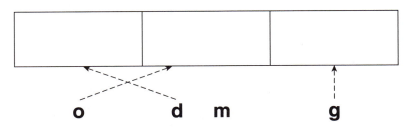

FIGURE 7–2   Example of Word Building Boxes with an Extraneous Letter from *How to Talk to Your Dog*

Initial Consonant Substitutions	Final Consonant Substitutions	Vowel Substitutions
dog ————————————————➤	do<u>t</u>	
<u>l</u>og		
<u>h</u>og		
fun		
<u>s</u>un		
<u>b</u>un		
<u>p</u>un ————————————————➤	pu<u>p</u> ————————————————➤	p<u>a</u>n
		p<u>i</u>n
		p<u>e</u>n
mad		
<u>s</u>ad		
<u>b</u>ad		
<u>h</u>ad ————————————————➤	ha<u>t</u> ————————————————➤	h<u>i</u>t
	ha<u>m</u> ————————————————➤	h<u>i</u>m
	ha<u>d</u> ————————————————➤	h<u>i</u>d
	ha<u>s</u> ————————————————➤	h<u>i</u>s

FIGURE 7–3   Examples of Word Building with Initial Consonants, Final Consonants, and Vowel Substitutions
Note: If the word being built requires a combination of letters to represent a phoneme, one of the boxes will need a dotted line. In the following example with "tell," the two "l's" are one grapheme representing one phoneme.

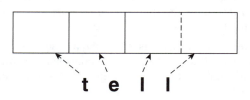

Further Reading

Frey, N., & Fisher, D. (2006). *Language arts workshop: Purposeful reading and writing instruction.* Columbus, OH: Pearson Prentice Hall.

Gipe, J. P. (2006). *Multiple paths to literacy: Assessment and differentiated instruction for diverse learners, K–12* (6th ed.). Upper Saddle River, NJ: Merrill/Prentice Hall.

Johns, J., & Lenski, S. D. (2001). *Improving reading: Strategies and resources* (3rd ed.). Dubuque, IA: Kendall/Hunt.

Multiple Word Meaning Matching Game

Strategy at a Glance: *Grade Levels 1–8*

When to Use	Grouping	Literature Type	Skill Areas
○ before reading	● individual	● narrative	● word recognition
○ during reading	● small group	○ expository	○ vocabulary
● after reading	○ whole class		● comprehension
	● center		○ writing

Purpose

To teach the literal and inferred meanings of multiple word meaning phrases

Literature Used

Play Ball, Amelia Bedelia, by Peggy Parish

When to Use

After reading

Description of Strategy

This strategy will help students seek literal and inferred meanings of phrases that have more than one meaning. The teacher writes these phrases from the story with multiple meanings on cards that are cut to be the same size. During the activity, the student will match the phrase on one card with its meaning from the story on another card.

Procedures for Use

1. *After* reading the story *Play Ball, Amelia Bedelia,* the teacher discusses the multiple word meaning phrases presented in the story. The teacher reviews the literal and inferred meanings of each phrase with students. For example, "Run home, Amelia Bedelia" in this story context means that Amelia should run to home base, not run to her house. By understanding the different meanings of the words, the reader can catch the humor of Amelia Bedelia stories, since Amelia always chooses the wrong or unintended definition of words or phrases.

2. Once readers seem to understand the phrases, the teacher sets cards face down on the table. The teacher then explains that the activity is similar to the game of matching.

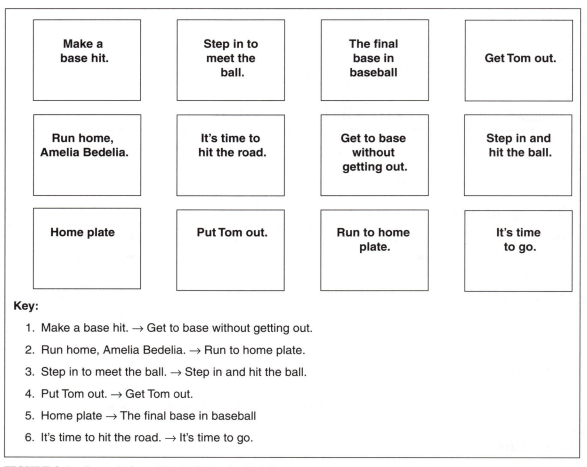

Make a base hit.	Step in to meet the ball.	The final base in baseball	Get Tom out.
Run home, Amelia Bedelia.	It's time to hit the road.	Get to base without getting out.	Step in and hit the ball.
Home plate	Put Tom out.	Run to home plate.	It's time to go.

Key:

1. Make a base hit. → Get to base without getting out.
2. Run home, Amelia Bedelia. → Run to home plate.
3. Step in to meet the ball. → Step in and hit the ball.
4. Put Tom out. → Get Tom out.
5. Home plate → The final base in baseball
6. It's time to hit the road. → It's time to go.

FIGURE 8–1   Example from *Play Ball, Amelia Bedelia*

3. The student picks up one card and reads what it says. The student flips over another card and reads what it says. Figure 8–1 illustrates possible phrases from *Play Ball, Amelia Bedelia* and their matching definitions.

4. If the two cards flipped are the phrase and the meaning of that phrase, as used in this story, the student keeps the two cards and continues to match.

    Example of two cards that match:
        Card 1: "Run home, Amelia Bedelia"
        Card 2: "Run to home plate"

If these two cards do not match, the student turns both cards over and repeats the process until two cards do match.

5. If students understand the concept of multiple word meanings, the teacher could apply it to a similar activity in a literacy center. The students might work in pairs and take turns matching the phrases.

Further Reading

Gipe, J. P. (2006). *Multiple paths to literacy: Assessment and differentiated instruction for diverse learners, K–12* (6th ed.). Upper Saddle River, NJ: Merrill/Prentice Hall.

Gunning, T. (2005). *Creating literacy instruction for all students* (5th ed.). Boston: Allyn & Bacon.

Word Detective Cards

Strategy at a Glance: *Grade Levels 1–6*

When to Use	Grouping	Literature Type	Skill Areas
● before reading	● individual	● narrative	● word recognition
● during reading	● small group	● expository	○ vocabulary
● after reading	● whole class		○ comprehension
	○ center		○ writing

Purpose

To help students become independent readers by learning strategies effective readers use to decode unknown words

Literature Used

The Puppy Who Wanted a Boy, by Jane Thayer

When to Use

Before, during, and after reading

Description of Strategy

Word detective cards present four word recognition strategies, one on each card, that efficient readers use when they come to an unknown word. Each of the four cards has directions for a reader to apply in decoding an unknown word by selecting from a variety of word attack competencies: context clues, structural analysis, phonics, and use of a dictionary.

Procedures for Use

1. The teacher selects a short passage with several words that the readers cannot automatically pronounce. In this example, the passage was from *The Puppy Who Wanted a Boy*. The words selected were "puppy," "dog," "I'd," and "Christmas." (See Figure 9–1.) The teacher writes individual sentences from the passage on sentence strips.

1	2	3	4
When I come to a word I don't know, I could read to the end of the sentence or paragraph.	When I come to a word I don't know, I could look for word parts with meaning.	When I come to a word I don't know, I could look for sounds I know.	When I come to a word I don't know, I could look it up in the dictionary.
(context clues)	(structural analysis)	(phonic analysis)	(dictionary)

One day Petey, who was a <u>puppy</u>, said to his mother, who was a <u>dog</u>. "<u>I'd</u> like to buy a boy for <u>Christmas</u>."

To figure out <u>puppy</u>, use detective card 1, 3, or 4.
To figure out <u>dog</u>, use detective card 1 or 3.
To figure out <u>I'd</u>, use detective card 1 or 2.
To figure out <u>Christmas</u>, use detective card 1.

FIGURE 9–1   Example of Word Detective Cards with *The Puppy Who Wanted a Boy*

2. The teacher asks the students whether they know what a detective is. If not, the teacher explains that a detective is someone who uses clues to figure out mysteries. The teacher tells the students that they will serve as word detectives and use clues to figure out the mystery of unknown words.

3. The teacher has the students read the individual sentences silently and underline any unknown words.

4. The teacher asks the students to reread the sentence out loud, saying "blank" when an unknown word appears.

5. The teacher shows the readers the first word detective card. The teacher reads the first word detective card to the students and asks whether the suggestion on that card will help to figure out the mystery of the word. (See Figure 9–1.)

6. If the first card does not help the student, the teacher will flip to the second card, then the third, then the fourth if necessary. **The order of the cards is very important!** The cards should be presented in the order in which efficient readers attempt to pronounce unknown words, starting with context clues, until the reader successfully reads the word. For example, if the unknown word is "puppy," the first detective card might be used. If the reader knows the word "dog" later in the sentence, the reader applies context clues to pronounce "puppy." The third detective card might be used next if the first clue didn't help, to break "puppy" into sound units, /pup/ /py/. Or the student might look the word "puppy" up in the dictionary, as the fourth card suggests.

7. The teacher may manipulate the cards to cover and uncover word parts to assist the students if they are dividing the word by structural or meaning units (the second card) or phonic or sound units (the third card).

8. The teacher will provide scaffolding as readers try to engage in the various word attack skills. If the student is trying to sound out the word "puppy," the teacher might help by showing the student how the word is divided into syllables and more easily pronounced as opposed to trying to blend isolated sounds.

9. Once the word has been identified, the teacher should ask the students whether the "guess" makes sense in the sentence.

Further Reading

Cooper, J. D. (2000). *Literacy*: *Helping children construct meaning* (4th ed.). Boston: Houghton Mifflin.

Tompkins, G. E. (2006). *Literacy for the 21st century: A balanced approach* (4th ed.). Upper Saddle River, NJ: Merrill/Prentice Hall.

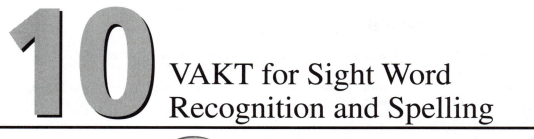 VAKT for Sight Word Recognition and Spelling

EL Beneficial when working with English learners

Purpose

To enhance sight word recognition, fluency, and correct spelling of words that are difficult to learn

Literature Used

Sector 7, by David Wiesner

When to Use

Before, during, and after reading

Description of Strategy

Developed by Grace Fernald and Helen Keller, VAKT (visual, auditory, kinesthetic, tactile) is an approach that improves recognition of sight words and increases spelling ability. The technique derives its power from the use of multiple modalities of learning. For a word that is difficult to establish as a sight word, the teacher shows the reader the word printed in letters large enough to be traced. The target word should have a raised or rough surface so that the reader can feel it as it is traced. A crayon works well for a raised, textured surface, or the word card may be inserted into a sleeve made by folding a mesh screen so that a rough surface is available for the reader to trace over. (See Figure 10–1.)

FIGURE 10–1   Example of a Mesh Screen
Sleeve and Word Card

An important consideration with this strategy is that the target word **not** be taught in isolation from a meaningful context. The word should derive from a narrative or expository passage students are reading. A further way to make the word meaningful is for the teacher or student to use it in a sentence during the following procedures.

Procedures for Use

1. To develop sight word fluency with a student, the teacher may select a book like *Sector 7,* a wordless picture storybook by David Wiesner. The book is shared with the student for a follow-up language experience story. (Refer to Strategy 5, Language Experience Approach for Sight Word Development.)

2. Once *Sector 7* has been shared and discussed, the student dictates to the teacher a short language experience story for a part of the book. The teacher and student then read the story in the shared reading mode of read *aloud, along, alone.* When the student independently reads the story *alone,* the teacher will note words that prove to be difficult for the student to pronounce automatically such as the word "where." The teacher could then employ VAKT as an *after* reading intervention to establish "where" as a sight word.

3. Using an index card, the teacher prints "where" in large letters for the student to trace:

The teacher pronounces the word and says it slowly as the student watches it being printed. Upon completing the printing, the teacher repeats the word in a normal voice and underlines it with a finger as the student looks at the word. The teacher next asks the student to look at the word and say it.

4. The teacher places the word card in a mesh screen to give it a textured surface over which to trace. (See Figure 10–1.) While looking at the word again, the student slowly pronounces "where" by stretching it out with the voice and at the same time tracing over the letters. Thus, the student sees the word, hears the word, and feels the word as part of the auditory, visual, and tactile components of VAKT.

5. The process continues until the student is able to write the word successfully from memory several times. The word card is then placed alphabetically in the reader's individual file box or "word bank" for later retrieval if it continues to prove troublesome when encountered in print.

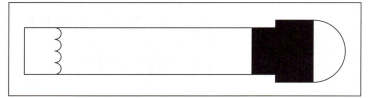

FIGURE 10–2   Example of a Water Pen with Sponge Tip

6. Had the reader needed additional practice with "where" or a more intense intervention to establish it as a sight word, the teacher could have tried a water pen. This is a hollow plastic tube with a small sponge on the end used for dampening seals on envelopes. (See Figure 10–2.)

This instrument aids the reader in remembering sight words by adding the kinesthetic component of VAKT. The student can trace the word on a chalkboard with the damp sponge tip of the water pen and thereby use large muscle movement as an additional learning modality. Again, the reader should slowly pronounce the word as each letter is traced. An alternative to a water pen for kinesthetic and tracing methods is any damp sponge.

Further Reading

Fernald, G. (1943). *Remedial techniques in basic school subjects.* New York: McGraw-Hill.

Gipe, J. P. (2006). *Multiple paths to literacy: Assessment and differentiated instruction for diverse learners, K–12* (6th ed.). Upper Saddle River, NJ: Merrill/Prentice Hall.

Harris, A. J., & Sipay, E. R. (1990). *How to increase reading ability: A guide to developmental and remedial methods* (9th ed.). New York: Longman.

Norton, T., & Land, B. L. (1992). A multisensory approach to teaching spelling in remedial English. *Teaching English in the Two-Year College, 19*, 192–195.

PART III

Vocabulary Strategies

Instruction in vocabulary is of critical importance and an undeniable part of developing comprehension of both narrative and expository text. Whereas Part II of this book focuses more on pronouncing or decoding as part of word recognition strategies, this part concentrates on providing native and nonnative English language learners scaffolding and sheltered instruction in understanding words. If students are reading and most of the words are new to them, they will struggle to construct anything meaningful about a text. Preview of any assignment is critical to determine potential vocabulary that may prove troublesome to readers in processing meaning. Teachers must find a variety of ways to expose students to such words as part of building background *before* reading. The preteaching of vocabulary will create opportunities for greater success in learners.

One way to develop vocabulary, whether English is the first or second language, is to assist learners in connecting their backgrounds to new words in a lesson. For instance, "surface current" may be an important term to know in a science lesson on the ocean. Some students may have heard about, seen a television or movie documentary on, or even been to, the ocean, but they may need assistance in understanding "surface current." As part of background or schema development, the teacher can connect the term to the movement of hot soup when someone blows on it across a bowl. Better yet, students could blow across a liquid in a bowl to observe a surface current firsthand. Such concrete experiences provide strong sheltered instruction for struggling readers, especially those whose first language is not English.

Another consideration in vocabulary development concerns terms for abstract concepts because their meanings are often difficult to define. Grammatical terms like "noun" and "verb" may be hard for learners to grasp if teachers only verbalize meanings that simply associate a term with a definition. A helpful way to develop understanding is to use graphic representations like word maps, thinking trees, concept circles, and semantic maps so that learners see connections and relationships among such words. Because these strategies also work well for words having concrete meanings and show their relationships to abstract concepts, this section offers a variety of these kinds of scaffolding activities for both types of terms that students will encounter.

The following graphic organizer (Figure III–1) illustrates the hierarchical connections among abstract and concrete vocabulary for the term "noun." "Noun" is the superordinate concept, whereas "abstract" and "concrete" are terms subordinate to it but coordinate with each other. "Abstract" then becomes the superordinate term for words like "goodness," "justice," and "fairness," which are coordinate with one another. The same holds true for the term "concrete" and its subordinate words like "animals," "things," and "people." Graphic organizers thus allow learners to visualize the deeper dimensions of vocabulary words through their relationships with one another.

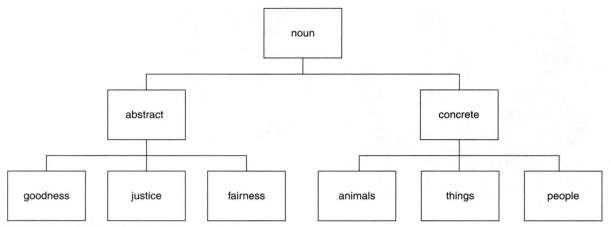

FIGURE III–1   Thinking Tree for Types of Nouns

11 Semantic Feature Analysis for Narrative and Informational Text

EL Beneficial when working with English learners

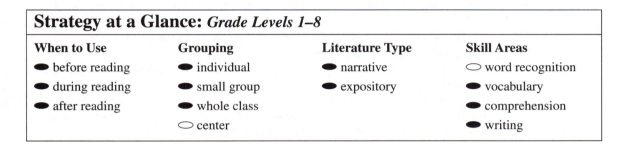

Strategy at a Glance: *Grade Levels 1–8*

When to Use	Grouping	Literature Type	Skill Areas
● before reading	● individual	● narrative	○ word recognition
● during reading	● small group	● expository	● vocabulary
● after reading	● whole class		● comprehension
	○ center		● writing

Purpose

To develop vocabulary proficiency by identifying word properties that may be similar or different from other words in a category and comparing and contrasting these concepts.

Literature Used

Pass the Fritters, Critters, by Cheryl Chapman (narrative)

Dinosaur Time, by Peggy Parish (expository)

When to Use

Before, during, and/or after reading

Description of Strategy

Semantic feature analysis uses a chart format to compare and contrast different characters, terms, or concepts from a book to help students with vocabulary development and a deeper understanding of concepts. A few words may be introduced *before* a selection is read, while others are added *during* reading, and still others *after* the passage or book is completed. The chart provides a helpful review of important concepts that the teacher wishes to emphasize to students. This process helps learners understand the deeper dimensions of the meanings of words.

Procedures for Use

1. A book or selection that is rich in terms related to one another works best. *Pass the Fritters, Critters,* by Cheryl Chapman, is a good example. *Dinosaur Time,* by Peggy Parish, has many vocabulary words that students can compare and contrast.

2. The teacher and students select key vocabulary from a book.

3. These items are then listed on the left-hand side of a grid or chart. In *Pass the Fritters, Critters,* students may select "muffin" and "cobbler." (See Figure 11–1.) In *Dinosaur Time,* the names of different dinosaurs may be listed on the left side of the grid (e.g., stegosaurus, diplodocus, ankylosaurus, etc.). (See Figure 11–2.)

4. With the teacher's assistance, students list the characteristics of selected terms and put these across the top of the grid.

5. Through student-teacher interactions, the items (foods or dinosaurs) from the book are then labeled as to which features they possess. A "+" indicates "yes" for a particular feature, while a "−" means "no" and a "?" means further investigation of other sources such as a dictionary or encyclopedia is necessary. A "+/−" means "yes" and "no," or that the food/dinosaur may or may not possess a given feature. Discussion among students or between the teacher and students is important to make sure that the learners understand that some terms are characterized by a feature and others are not.

6. Additional names and features may be placed on the grid as further reading and enrichment occurs.

7. Once the grid is completed, it serves as a review of the topic or unit of study, as can be seen from the samples of semantic feature analysis provided in Figures 11–1 and 11–2.

Alternate Idea

The basic chart may be created, and the concepts, attributes, and symbols (+, −, ?, +/−) may be added to the chart using self-stick notes. This idea is especially effective for tactile/kinesthetic

Food	Attributes				
	Sweet	**Made with Fruit**	**Vegetable**	**Eaten Raw**	**Requires Utensil**
fritters	+	+	−	−	−
cantalope	+	+	−	+	+/−
muffin	+	+	−	−	−
eclair	+	−	−	−	−
cobbler	+	+	−	−	+
honey	+	−	−	+	+/−
carrot	−	−	+	+/−	+/−
salami	−	−	−	+?	+/−
cider	+	+	−	+	+(glass)

+ = yes
− = no
? = need for further study
+/− = yes and no

FIGURE 11–1   Example for *Pass and Fritters, Critters*

Dinosaurs	Attributes			
	Meat-eater	**Plant-eater**	**Smooth Body**	**Rough Body**
stegosaurus	−	+	−	+
diplodocus	−	+	+	−
ankylosaurus	?	?	−	+
brontosaurus	−	+	−	+
compsognathus	+	−	+	−
teratosaurus	+	−	+	−
anatosaurus	?	?	−	+
ornithominus	+	+	+	−

+ = yes
− = no
? = need for further study
+/− = yes and no

FIGURE 11–2   Example for *Dinosaur Time*

learners. The chart may eventually be placed in a center, and the self-stick notes removed for the students to replace. Learners needing more practice or reinforcement will benefit from this idea.

Further Reading

Cooper, J. D. (2000). *Literacy: Helping children construct meaning* (4th ed.). Boston: Houghton Mifflin.

Cooter, R. B., Jr., & Flynt, E. S. (1996). *Teaching reading in the content areas: Developing content literacy for all students.* Englewood Cliffs, NJ: Prentice Hall.

Cunningham, P., & Allington, R. (1994). *Classrooms that work.* New York: HarperCollins.

Cunningham, P. M., Moore, S. A., Cunningham, J. W., & Moore, D. W. (1995). *Reading and writing in elementary classrooms: Strategies and observations* (3rd ed.). White Plains, NY: Longman.

Frey, N., & Fisher, D. (2006). *Language arts workshop: Purposeful reading and writing instruction.* Columbus, OH: Pearson Prentice Hall.

Gipe, J. P. (2006). *Multiple paths to literacy: Assessment and differentiated instruction for diverse learners, K–12* (6th ed.). Upper Saddle River, NJ: Merrill/Prentice Hall.

Graves, M., Juel, C., & Graves, B. (1998). *Teaching reading in the 21st century.* Needham Heights, MA: Allyn & Bacon.

Gunning, T. (2005). *Creating literacy instruction for all students* (5th ed.). Boston: Allyn & Bacon.

Harris, A. J., & Sipay, E. R. (1990). *How to increase reading ability: A guide to developmental and remedial methods* (9th ed.). New York: Longman.

Johns, J., & Lenski, S. D. (2001). *Improving reading: Strategies and resources* (3rd ed.). Dubuque, IA: Kendall/Hunt.

Reutzel, D. R., & Cooter, R. (2000). *Teaching children to read: Putting the pieces together* (3rd ed.). Columbus, OH: Merrill.

Vacca, R. T., & Vacca, J. A. L. (2005). *Content area reading: Literacy and learning across the curriculum* (8th ed.). Boston: Allyn & Bacon.

12 Concept of Definition or Word Map

 EL Beneficial when working with English learners

Strategy at a Glance: *Grade Levels 4–8*			
When to Use	**Grouping**	**Literature Type**	**Skill Areas**
● before reading	○ individual	● narrative	○ word recognition
● during reading	● small group	● expository	● vocabulary
● after reading	● whole class		● comprehension
	○ center		● writing

Purpose

To activate background and expand vocabulary through an examination of the components of an analytical definition

Literature Used

Follow the Drinking Gourd, by Jeanette Winter

When to Use

Before, during, and/or after reading

Description of Strategy

Concept of definition, or word mapping, is a vocabulary development strategy that activates prior knowledge *before* reading or expands knowledge *during* and *after* reading. The technique uses a visual representation to show specific parts of a vocabulary concept. When the strategy is used *before* reading, key concept words must be selected prior to reading the literature selection. An example of the components associated with a word map is shown in Figure 12–1. *Before* reading, the teacher and students should discuss the vocabulary word, or key concept, and what the students know about it, such as some of its characteristics or some examples. This discussion activates background knowledge. Together, the teacher and students make a list of properties or examples related to the key concept. Some of the characteristics or examples can be

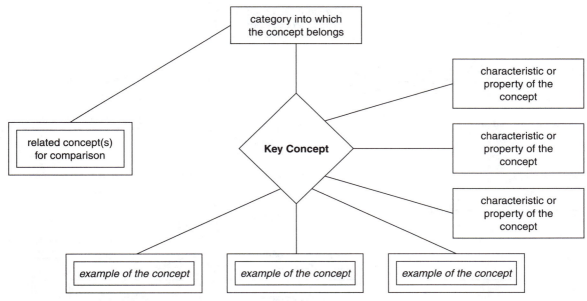

FIGURE 12–1 Example of Components Associated with a Word Map

recorded on the map. *During* reading, these may be added to or changed. *After* reading, the teacher and students decide whether the definition is still incomplete and may search other sources for further information to complete the components of the definition. The following procedures illustrate the strategy for a children's book that could be used with intermediate- and middle-grade social studies.

Procedures for Use

1. The teacher introduces a key concept used in the book, *Follow the Drinking Gourd.* In this example, the concept is "slaves." This word is recorded in the center of the map. (Refer to the completed word map in Figure 12–2.)

2. The teacher and students next identify the category in which the concept "slaves" belongs. For instance, slaves may be classified as workers. "Workers" then goes at the top of the map.

3. Comparisons can now be made between "slaves" and similar concepts by listing other examples of "workers," such as "carpenters" and "farmers." These examples go to the left of the map as "Related Concept(s) for Comparison."

4. The teacher and students brainstorm and list characteristics or properties of "slaves." Examples may include "lived and worked on plantations," "abused and beaten," and "did not have freedom." Reader responses go to the right of the map in boxes labeled "Characteristics or Properties of the Concept."

5. Students next try to think of illustrations of "slaves." These may include such examples as "cotton pickers," "domestic (or house) workers," "field hands," and "skilled laborers." These terms go at the bottom of the map in the boxes labeled "Examples of the Concept" and could be subdivided further. "House workers" could be divided, for instance, into "butlers," "maids," "cooks," and so forth.

6. As a follow-up, the concept may be formally written by having students arrange the map into a definition sentence or paragraph (in this instance, "slaves") based on the information given in the map. Responses and final definitions will vary based on background and further reading.

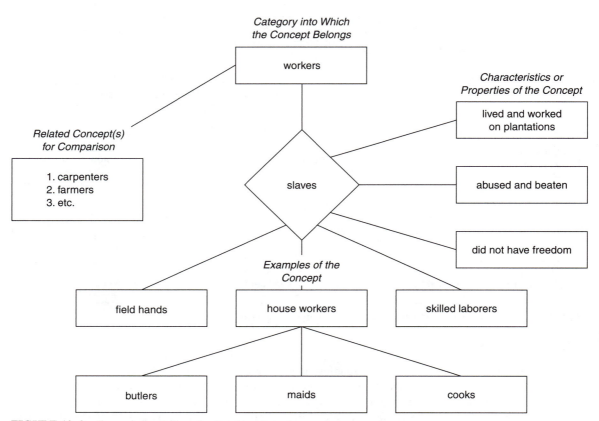

FIGURE 12–2   Example for *Follow the Drinking Gourd*

7. In summary, the basic process for concept of definition is to *list* ideas about a concept, *group* the ideas, and *label* the ideas as "Characteristics or Properties of the Concept," "Examples of the Concept," or "Related Concept(s) for Comparison."

Further Reading

Cooper, J. D. (2000). *Literacy: Helping children construct meaning* (4th ed.). Boston: Houghton Mifflin.

Frey, N., & Fisher, D. (2006). *Language arts workshop: Purposeful reading and writing instruction.* Columbus, OH: Pearson Prentice Hall.

Gipe, J. P. (2006). *Multiple paths to literacy: Assessment and differentiated instruction for diverse learners, K–12* (6th ed.). Upper Saddle River, NJ: Merrill/Prentice Hall.

Harris, A. J., & Sipay, E. R. (1990). *How to increase reading ability: A guide to developmental and remedial methods* (9th ed.). New York: Longman.

Johns, J., & Lenski, S. D. (2001). *Improving reading: Strategies and resources* (3rd ed.). Dubuque, IA: Kendall/Hunt.

Reutzel, D. R., & Cooter, R. (2000). *Teaching children to read: Putting the pieces together* (3rd ed.). Columbus, OH: Merrill.

Ruddell, R. B., & Ruddell, M. R. (1995). *Teaching children to read and write: Becoming an influential teacher.* Boston: Allyn & Bacon.

Tierney, R. J., & Readence, J. E. (2000). *Reading strategies and practices: A compendium* (5th ed.). Boston: Allyn & Bacon.

Vacca, J. A. L., Vacca, R. T., & Gove, M. K. (2000). *Reading and learning to read* (4th ed.). New York: Addison Wesley Longman.

Vacca, R. T., & Vacca, J. A. L. (2005). *Content area reading: Literacy and learning across the curriculum* (8th ed.). Boston: Allyn & Bacon.

Thinking Tree

EL Beneficial when working with English learners

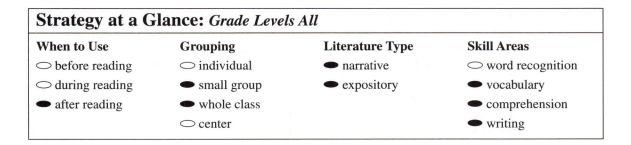

Strategy at a Glance: *Grade Levels All*

When to Use	Grouping	Literature Type	Skill Areas
○ before reading	○ individual	● narrative	○ word recognition
○ during reading	● small group	● expository	● vocabulary
● after reading	● whole class		● comprehension
	○ center		● writing

Purpose

To show the hierarchical relationships among vocabulary terms or among main ideas and details through the use of a graphic organizer

Literature Used

The News about Dinosaurs, by Patricia Lauber

When to Use

After reading

Description of Strategy

A thinking tree is an instructional tool to help students organize information into categories that are hierarchically arranged. Depending on learner needs and abilities, thinking trees can be modified. A thinking tree starts with a broad category at the top of the tree chart. Students can select this category, be supplied with the category, or choose the category from a given concept bank. As the tree chart moves down, the categories get more specific. Each category describes in greater detail the category above it. The tree chart also expands horizontally each time it moves down. Thus, a thinking tree contains superordinate, subordinate, and coordinate items. The chart may initially provide some of the superordinate, subordinate, and coordinate concepts so that students fill in the remaining items themselves, or students may choose from a concept bank provided by the teacher. The teacher decides how the thinking trees will be filled in and how much scaffolding, or assistance, is needed.

Procedures for Use

1. The literature selected for this thinking tree is *The News about Dinosaurs.*

2. *After* the literature has been read either in an independent or a shared mode such as read *aloud, along,* or *alone,* the teacher provides a random list of topics that students later arrange hierarchically into a thinking tree. Alternatively, the teacher may guide the students in generating a list of concepts from the text.

3. The concepts, whether from the teacher, from students, or from both, are then arranged into a thinking tree that shows superordinate, subordinate, or coordinate relationships. For less able students, the tree chart may be provided. Others may create their own. The degree of scaffolding provided by the teacher is dependent upon the individual needs of learners.

4. For *The News about Dinosaurs,* the teacher has provided the thinking tree and a list of terms in a concept bank. (See Figure 13–1.) The superordinate concept is "dinosaurs." Subordinate to it and coordinate with each other are "plant-eaters" and "meat-eaters." Then subordinate to these and coordinate with one another are examples of different dinosaurs.

5. From the concept bank, students hierarchically order the terms from *The News about Dinosaurs.* This work may be done independently, cooperatively, or with teacher guidance. Moreover, the teacher may have some sections of the thinking tree already completed if this degree of scaffolding is necessary for particular students. (See Figure 13–1.)

6. Depending on the student, a thinking tree may continue to expand or stop after one or two subordinate levels are completed.

7. The teacher may give several examples of thinking trees to lead students eventually to create their own thinking trees. Figure 13–2 provides a variation of Figure 13–1.

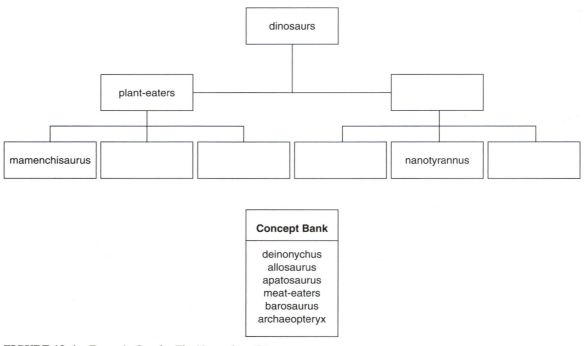

FIGURE 13–1   Example One for *The News about Dinosaurs*
Note: This thinking tree has some of the categories filled in to provide greater scaffolding to help the students decide what should go in the rest of the category boxes. This thinking tree also has a concept bank. Students will fill in the category boxes with words or names from this randomly ordered list.

Concept Bank

plant-eaters
mamenchisaurus
deinonychus
meat-eaters
nanotyrannus
albertosaurus
camarasaurus
apatosaurus

FIGURE 13–2   Example Two for *The News about Dinosaurs*

Note: Some thinking trees may be like this one. The broad category is given, and the remaining thinking tree boxes have to be filled in by the student with words from the concept box. This type of thinking tree requires a higher level of application than does the first example. Thinking trees can expand.

Further Reading

Cooper, J. D. (2000). *Literacy: Helping children construct meaning* (4th ed.). Boston: Houghton Mifflin.

Cooter, R. B., Jr., & Flynt, E. S. (1996). *Teaching reading in the content areas: Developing content literacy for all students*. Englewood Cliffs, NJ: Prentice Hall.

Graves, M., Juel, C., & Graves, B. (1998). *Teaching reading in the 21st century*. Needham Heights, MA: Allyn & Bacon.

Gunning, T. (2005). *Creating literacy instruction for all students* (5th ed.). Boston: Allyn & Bacon.

Johns, J., & Lenski, S. D. (2001). *Improving reading: Strategies and resources* (3rd ed.). Dubuque, IA: Kendall/Hunt.

Reutzel, D. R., & Cooter, R. (2000). *Teaching children to read: Putting the pieces together* (3rd ed.). Columbus, OH: Merrill.

Vacca, R. T., & Vacca, J. A. L. (2005). *Content area reading: Literacy and learning across the curriculum* (8th ed.). Boston: Allyn & Bacon.

14 Semantic Mapping or Webbing

EL Beneficial when working with English learners

Strategy at a Glance: *Grade Levels All*

When to Use	Grouping	Literature Type	Skill Areas
● before reading	○ individual	● narrative	○ word recognition
● during reading	● small group	● expository	● vocabulary
● after reading	● whole class		● comprehension
	○ center		● writing

Purpose

To organize information through a graphic depiction of words, concepts, or ideas and to demonstrate their relationship to one another

Literature Used

I Can Be a Zookeeper, by James P. Rowan

When to Use

Before, during, and/or after reading

Description of Strategy

Semantic mapping or webbing is a visual organizational technique that displays ideas according to the way they relate to one another categorically. It may be used *before* reading to preview key vocabulary and to focus student attention on important concepts that will appear in the text. It may also be used *during* and *after* reading to reinforce or to expand vocabulary and thereby increase comprehension. Usually, a key concept is selected by the teacher and discussed to build or activate the prior background of learners. They may add characteristics of the key concept to the map. *During* reading, these may be further added or taken from the map as necessary. *After* reading, the teacher and students complete the map by adding any relevant information obtained from the literature. The steps that follow suggest how semantic mapping improves comprehension of *I Can Be a Zookeeper*.

Procedures for Use

1. The teacher introduces a key term in *I Can Be a Zookeeper,* in this instance "zookeeper," which is written in the center of the map.

2. *Before* reading, the teacher may read the title of the book and have students hypothesize what information it will contain. *I Can Be a Zookeeper* contains information about the job of a zookeeper. Students will learn some things that a zookeeper does. They can come up with a title for the semantic map. A good title for this map might be "Jobs of a Zookeeper." If students already know some of the jobs of a zookeeper, they may fill in some of the circles surrounding the term.

3. The teacher will read the book and direct students to pay close attention to the descriptions given. They clearly outline several jobs of a zookeeper.

4. Once the book is read, students will look at the information already placed in the map and will decide whether it is correct and should stay or whether it is incorrect and needs to be omitted or modified. Students will then recall as much information as possible from the book and fill in the remainder of the concept map.

5. After the information has been listed, the teacher should encourage learners to revise the map by grouping information into labeled subcategories with appropriate supporting details. Thus, semantic mapping will help students recall and organize information from the text as they develop vocabulary and classifying abilities. In Figure 14–1, the ideas

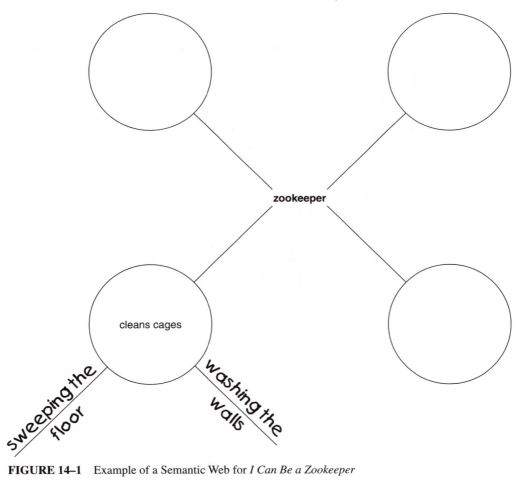

Jobs of a Zookeeper

zookeeper

cleans cages

sweeping the floor

washing the walls

FIGURE 14–1 Example of a Semantic Web for *I Can Be a Zookeeper* of "washing the walls" and "sweeping the floor" are attached to a larger category, "cleans cages."

6. The semantic web for *I Can Be a Zookeeper* can also be created as a fishbone to show students another way to organize the same ideas.

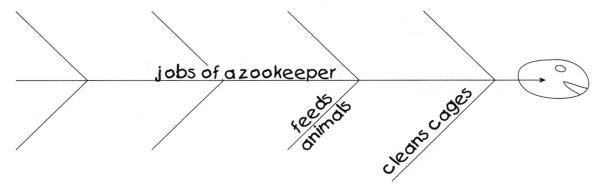

7. Using these kinds of graphic organizers, whether semantic mapping or a fishbone, gives learners a way to outline information as a prewriting activity for a written summary.

Further Reading

Cooper, J. D. (2000). *Literacy: Helping children construct meaning* (4th ed.). Boston: Houghton Mifflin.

Cunningham, P., & Allington, R. (1994). *Classrooms that work.* New York: HarperCollins.

Graves, M., Juel, C., & Graves, B. (1998). *Teaching reading in the 21st century.* Needham Heights, MA: Allyn & Bacon.

Gunning, T. (2005). *Creating literacy instruction for all students* (5th ed.). Boston: Allyn & Bacon.

Harris, A. J., & Sipay, E. R. (1990). *How to increase reading ability: A guide to developmental and remedial methods* (9th ed.). New York: Longman.

Johns, J., & Lenski, S. D. (2001). *Improving reading: Strategies and resources* (3rd ed.). Dubuque, IA: Kendall/Hunt.

Reutzel, D. R., & Cooter, R. (2000). *Teaching children to read: Putting the pieces together* (3rd ed.). Columbus, OH: Merrill.

Ruddell, R. B., & Ruddell, M. R. (1995). *Teaching children to read and write: Becoming an influential teacher.* Boston: Allyn & Bacon.

Vacca, J. A. L., Vacca, R. T., & Gove, M. K. (2000). *Reading and learning to read* (4th ed.). New York: Addison Wesley Longman.

Vacca, R. T., & Vacca, J. A. L. (2005). *Content area reading: Literacy and learning across the curriculum* (8th ed.). Boston: Allyn & Bacon.

Magic Squares

EL Beneficial when working with English learners

Strategy at a Glance: *Grade Levels All*

When to Use	Grouping	Literature Type	Skill Areas
○ before reading	● individual	● narrative	○ word recognition
○ during reading	● small group	● expository	● vocabulary
● after reading	○ whole class		● comprehension
	○ center		○ writing

Purpose

To review key vocabulary terms for a lesson or unit of study whether based on narrative or expository text

Literature Used

South Carolina: Its History and Geography, by Paul Horne, Jr.

When to Use

After reading

Description of Strategy

Magic squares is a vocabulary reinforcement activity that gives additional exposure to terms *after* reading is completed. Students match key vocabulary words to their correct definitions. The activity, however, goes beyond a humdrum matching exercise in that it is like a game in which students record answers in a magic square grid made up of boxes like the one in Figure 15–1.

Each letter in the grid represents a term where learners write the number of the definition that matches. If they have correctly completed the activity, the numbers of the definitions, when added

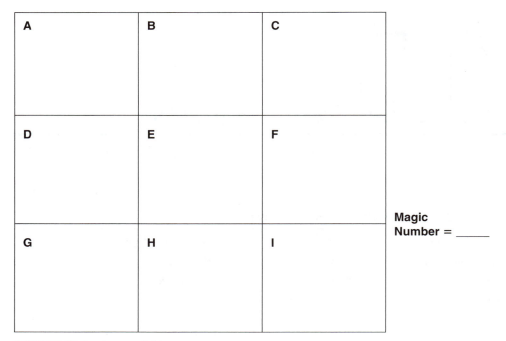

FIGURE 15–1   Answer Grid

across each row and down each column, will equal the same "magic" number. Thus, the activity allows students to check their work for the accuracy of the matches. Magic squares work well with individual students or in small collaborative learning groups. The latter is particularly effective in reinforcing vocabulary words as students read the terms and definitions and engage in talking about them and hearing them through cooperative discussion.

Procedures for Use

1. The teacher should decide, *before* a lesson or unit is taught, the key terms that students should know and that support important learning outcomes.

2. The teacher should preview some of the terms *before,* and call attention to them *during,* the lesson to provide multiple exposures. This process is necessary for especially difficult concepts like the state motto of South Carolina, "Dum Spiro Spero."

3. *After* reading, reinforcement of terms and definitions for further exposure can occur with the magic squares activity. The example for *South Carolina: Its History and Geography,* an elementary social studies text, provides a review for nine key terms related to facts and symbols associated with South Carolina. (See Figure 15–4.)

4. To prevent the teacher from having to invent various magic square combinations, a time-consuming endeavor, additional ones are provided in Figure 15–2. The number with the single asterisk under each grid represents how many definitions must be foils, while the number with the double asterisk is the magic number that each row and column should sum up to if the exercise has been completed correctly.

5. Further magic square grids can be easily made by taking any one of the previous patterns and reconfiguring rows or columns. (See Figures 15–3 through 15–5.)

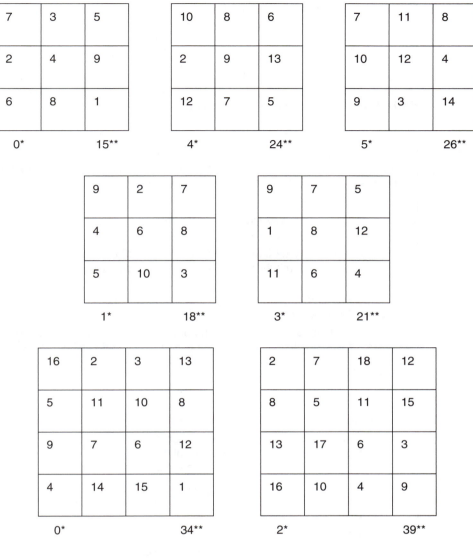

7	3	5
2	4	9
6	8	1

0*　　　　15**

10	8	6
2	9	13
12	7	5

4*　　　　24**

7	11	8
10	12	4
9	3	14

5*　　　　26**

9	2	7
4	6	8
5	10	3

1*　　　　18**

9	7	5
1	8	12
11	6	4

3*　　　　21**

16	2	3	13
5	11	10	8
9	7	6	12
4	14	15	1

0*　　　　　　34**

2	7	18	12
8	5	11	15
13	17	6	3
16	10	4	9

2*　　　　　　39**

19	2	15	23	6
25	8	16	4	12
1	14	22	10	18
7	20	3	11	24
13	21	9	17	5

0*　　　　　　　　65**

*foils for answer column with definitions
**magic number

FIGURE 15–2　Magic Square Combinations

10	8	6
2	9	13
12	7	5

→

12	5	7
10	6	8
2	13	9

→

8	10	6
9	2	13
7	12	5

FIGURE 15–3 More Magic Square Combinations

Directions: We have just finished a unit about facts and symbols associated with South Carolina. We have covered a lot of information, and this activity can help you remember some of the vocabulary words from the unit.

Directions:

1. Look at the lists below. One list has vocabulary words from our unit. The other list has the definitions for the words.

2. Do you see the square at the bottom of the page? In the square, there are nine smaller squares with letters in them. The letters stand for the vocabulary words in our unit.

3. Write the number at the definition that matches in the proper square. Look at the example before you begin work.

4. The rows that go up and down and from side to side should all add up to be the same number. If this happens, you have probably gotten all of the definitions right.

5. Do your best!

Example:

Vocabulary List
A. Dog
B. Cat

Definition List
1. an animal that barks
2. an animal that meows

Exercise:

Vocabulary List

A. capital
B. Carolina jessamine
C. palmetto
D. "dum spiro spero"
E. milk
F. symbol
G. shag
H. Carolina wren
I. state flag

Definition List

1. Myrtle Beach
2. state motto
3. state song
4. state stone
5. designed by Colonel William Moultrie
6. state tree
7. state bird
8. state flower
9. state drink
10. where state government is located
11. is located on the coast
12. state dance
13. one thing that stands for another

A	B	C
D	E	F
G	H	I

Magic Number = _____

FIGURE 15–4 Example for *South Carolina: Its History and Geography*

Magic Square
Answer Key

A	B	C
10	8	6
D	E	F
2	9	13
G	H	I
12	7	5

Magic Number = <u>24</u>

*Definition numbers 1, 3, 4, and 11 are foils
or incorrect answers.

FIGURE 15–5   Magic Square Answer Key

Further Reading

Vacca, R. T., & Vacca, J. A. L. (2005). *Content area reading: Literacy and learning across the curriculum* (8th ed.). Boston: Allyn & Bacon.

16 Context Puzzles

EL Beneficial when working with English learners

Strategy at a Glance: *Grade Levels All*

When to Use	Grouping	Literature Type	Skill Areas
○ before reading	● individual	● narrative	● word recognition
○ during reading	● small group	● expository	● vocabulary
● after reading	○ whole class		● comprehension
	○ center		○ writing

Purpose

To reinforce knowledge of important vocabulary by having students use words in a meaningful context

Literature Used

Practical Record Keeping and Bookkeeping, by Harold Baron, Solomon C. Steinfeld, and Robert A. Schultheis

Art in Action, by Guy Hubbard

When to Use

After reading

Description of Strategy

Context puzzles are a variation of word puzzles. Unlike word puzzles, however, which give students definitions as clues, context puzzles require learners to apply vocabulary knowledge in a functional context. Students must use syntactic and semantic clues to determine the correct answer. Context puzzles are formatted as fill-in-the-blank activities and may consist of one sentence for each term or several connected sentences from a passage rich in vocabulary, particularly technical words found in content texts of an expository nature. The latter is a modified cloze puzzle having deletions of subject matter words as opposed to an *n*th (e.g., fifth) word deletion pattern. The teacher may scaffold these activities through letter clues; structural clues such as syllables, prefixes, and suffixes; or a blank space for each omitted letter of the term in question. Context puzzles may be completed in collaborative learning teams that require students to talk about terms, hear them, read them, and write them for additional reinforcement of learning.

Procedures for Use

1. A passage containing important vocabulary, often many technical terms, is ideal for a context puzzle to provide learners with review and practice using the words *after* reading. Examples from a unit on balancing a checkbook from *Practical Record Keeping and Bookkeeping* for a secondary business class and a unit on one-color collages from *Art in Action* for fifth-grade art are provided in Figures 16–1 and 16–2, respectively.

2. For the business puzzle, the teacher uses individual sentences that require learners to place each term in a meaningful context. The teacher must be sure that the sentences do indeed contain context clues. Otherwise, students will have too great a difficulty with the task because they cannot decipher the meanings of terms unless the context is adequate. The example for *Practical Record Keeping and Bookkeeping* shown in Figure 16–1 contains scaffolding with blanks for omitted letters and with some letters filled in. A word bank could also aid less able learners.

3. With the modified cloze puzzle for art, the teacher types a one-inch blank for each omitted word. This way, students must answer based on context, not on typographical clues. Unlike a cloze procedure used as a *before* reading background assessment, a modified cloze puzzle does not employ a random deletion pattern for every *n*th word (usually every fifth word). Instead, this activity deletes only key vocabulary with which students need additional practice. The teacher could further scaffold this puzzle through letter, syllable, or affix clues in the blanks or through a concept bank from which students select answers. It all depends on the ability of the learners as to how much guidance the teacher gives them.

Directions: Use the sentences below, which contain clues for the meanings of words that we have from our unit on balancing a checkbook. Additional clues are provided with blanks for letters omitted from each term. In some cases, missing letters are given.

1. Banks can require customers to pay a s __ r __ __ __ __ e   c h __ __ __ __ __ for handling their deposits or for paying for their checks.

2. Sam went to his bank and made a __ __ t h __ __ __ __ __ l of $500 in cash to pay for a new paint job on his truck.

3. In order to __ __ __ __ __ __ i l e her checkbook with her bank statement, Susy had to determine that the balance in her checkbook matched her bank statement.

4. Susy used her __ __ __ __   __ __ c o n __ __ __ __ __ __ __ __ n   s t __ __ __ __ __ __ t to see whether her check to the grocery store matched the amount recorded on her monthly statement from her bank.

5. When Jim received his paycheck in September, he recorded the amount in his checkbook. However, his bank statement for August did not show the amount of this __ __ __ s t __ __ __ i n g   d __ __ __ __ __ __ .

6. On June 1, Jim wrote a check for $30 to Home Depot for gardening tools he had purchased. His bank statement, dated May 28, will not show his __ __ __ __ __ __ e d   b __ __ __ __ __ __ for his June check.

Key:

1. service charge
2. withdrawal
3. reconcile

4. bank reconciliation statement
5. outstanding deposit
6. adjusted balance

FIGURE 16–1   Example for *Practical Record Keeping and Bookkeeping*

Directions: You have studied the section titled "One-Color Collage." From your text, you should have learned terms related to your reading as well as the artwork you created in class. You are required to fill in the missing words in this passage. Carefully read the content of the sentences because they contain clues to your answers.

Have you ever looked at the world through red-tinted glasses? Everything seems to show up as [1]____ of red. When something appears to be one color, we say that it is [2]____ . Colors, or [3]____ , can be changed in many ways. Adding black, white, or gray is a common way to change a color. You can add black to a color and make a [4]____ . You can add white and make a [5]____ . When you add gray to a color, you make a [6]____ . Pablo Picasso painted an all-blue painting called "The Blind Man's Meal." By repeating and varying the same color, you were asked to create a [7]____ . This is a [8]____ design made of materials such as paper and fabrics glued to a flat background. In creating your non-objective art, you were asked to use [9]____ shapes.

Key:
1. variations
2. monochrome or monochromatic
3. hues
4. shade
5. tint
6. tone
7. collage
8. two-dimensional
9. geometric or free-form

FIGURE 16–2   Example for *Art in Action*

Further Reading

Cunningham, P. (2000). *Phonics they use* (3rd ed.). New York: Longman.

Gunning, T. (2005). *Creating literacy instruction for all students* (5th ed.). Boston: Allyn & Bacon.

Johns, J., & Lenski, S. D. (2001). *Improving reading: Strategies and resources* (3rd ed.). Dubuque, IA: Kendall/Hunt.

Reutzel, D. R., & Cooter, R. (2000). *Teaching children to read: Putting the pieces together* (3rd ed.). Columbus, OH: Merrill.

Ruddell, R. B., & Ruddell, M. R. (1995). *Teaching children to read and write: Becoming an influential teacher.* Boston: Allyn & Bacon.

Tierney, R. J., & Readence, J. E. (2000). *Reading strategies and practices: A compendium* (5th ed.). Boston: Allyn & Bacon.

Vacca, J. A. L., Vacca, R. T., & Gove, M. K. (2000). *Reading and learning to read* (4th ed.). New York: Addison Wesley Longman.

Vacca, R. T., & Vacca, J. A. L. (2005). *Content area reading: Literacy and learning across the curriculum* (8th ed.). Boston: Allyn & Bacon.

17 Closed and Open Word Sorts

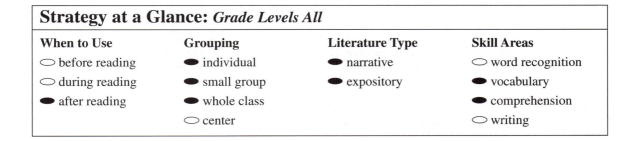

Strategy at a Glance: *Grade Levels All*

When to Use	Grouping	Literature Type	Skill Areas
○ before reading	● individual	● narrative	○ word recognition
○ during reading	● small group	● expository	● vocabulary
● after reading	● whole class		● comprehension
	○ center		○ writing

Purpose

To reinforce interrelationships among words and their meanings from an instructional unit so that students understand categories, properties, and examples of important terms

Literature Used

Holt Life Science, by Patricia A. Watkins and Glenn K. Leto
The Story of America, by John A. Garraty

When to Use

After reading

Description of Strategy

Students sort terms into different categorical groups through determining common features among their meanings. In closed sorts, the teacher provides the categories under which students are to group a given set of words. Here, the thinking is convergent and based on deduction. In open sorts, the students themselves group the given words into logical categories that they create based on previous reading and study. With open sorts, the thinking may be divergent since the word groupings are based on induction.

Procedures for Use

1. For a closed sort, the teacher searches the chapter, "Support and Movement," from *Holt Life Science* for middle-level learners and determines the key vocabulary on which to focus attention *before* and *during* reading. These words become the concept bank for students in the closed sort reinforcement of vocabulary *after* reading. (See Figure 17–1.) The same process applies to a senior high open sort activity for the chapter, "The Civil War," from *The Story of America.* (See Figure 17–2.) Both activities use a graphic organizer (i.e., a hierarchical array) to show connections among classes, properties, and examples.

2. In the closed sort, the teacher determines the major categories students will use to group the words and supplies these categories in the concept bank. In the one for *Holt Life Science,* the superordinate classes are "skeletal system" and "muscular system." Subordinate categories for "muscular system" have also been listed and are "skeletal muscles," "smooth muscles," and "cardiac muscles." For scaffolding, two of these are written on the graphic organizer. Thus, the teacher has completed part of the closed sort and requires students to complete the remainder from the concept bank.

Directions: Choose the correct word or phrase from the concept bank below for each empty space on the graphic organizer. Only one word or phrase belongs in each space. Remember to write neatly.

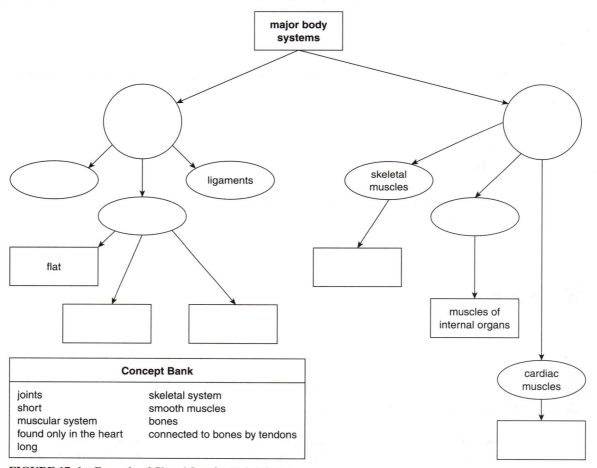

Concept Bank	
joints	skeletal system
short	smooth muscles
muscular system	bones
found only in the heart	connected to bones by tendons
long	

FIGURE 17–1   Example of Closed Sort for *Holt Life Science*

Note: This graphic organizer has some of the categories filled in to provide greater scaffolding to help students decide what should go in the rest of the category boxes. This graphic organizer also has a concept bank. Students will fill in the category boxes with words or names from this randomly ordered list.

Directions: Below is a concept bank of names and battles from the chapter on the Civil War. Classify the vocabulary terms by arranging them into logical groups. Be prepared to show the logic behind your thinking.

Concept Bank:

General William T. Sherman
Battle of Fredericksburg
The Union
General Thomas J. "Stonewall" Jackson
General Pierre Beauregard
Battle of Vicksburg
Battle of Antietam

General Ulysses S. Grant
Battle of Gettysburg
Second Battle of Bull Run
General Robert E. Lee
General George B. McClellan
Battle of Chancellorsville
The Confederate States of America

Answer Key:

The following categories are logical groupings. However, students may vary these somewhat. For example, students may classify generals under battles in which they fought as acceptable categories.

The Confederate States of America

Generals:
General Robert E. Lee
General Pierre Beauregard
General Thomas J. "Stonewall" Jackson

Battles Won by the Confederacy:
Second Battle of Bull Run
Battle of Fredericksburg
Battle of Chancellorsville

The Union

Generals:
General William T. Sherman
General Ulysses S. Grant
General George B. McClellan

Battles Won by the Union:
Battle of Gettysburg
Battle of Vicksburg
Battle of Antietam

FIGURE 17–2   Example One of Open Sort for *The Story of America*

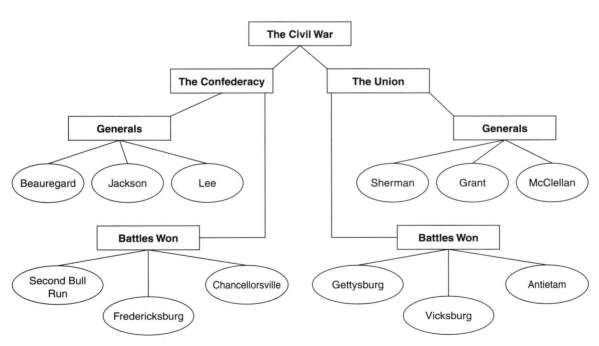

FIGURE 17–3   Example Two of Open Sort for *The Story of America*
Note: This open sort graphic organizer represents another way the teacher might require students to categorize the terms from the concept bank. The only requirement is that the students must be able to logically justify their arrangement of ideas in the hierarchical array. (See Strategy 13, Thinking Tree, pages 47–49.)

3. In the open sort for *The Story of America,* only the vocabulary list is provided. Students may group the words under logical headings as in Figure 17–2, or they may create a graphic organizer to visually represent the relationships among the concepts as in Figure 17–3.

4. Both closed and open sorts have an added advantage in developing reading comprehension in that they help students understand main idea-detail relationships, an essential component of hierarchical order.

Further Reading

Graves, M., Juel, C., & Graves, B. (1998). *Teaching reading in the 21st century.* Needham Heights, MA: Allyn & Bacon.

Gunning, T. (2005). *Creating literacy instruction for all students* (5th ed.). Boston: Allyn & Bacon.

Johns, J., & Lenski, S. D. (2001). *Improving reading: Strategies and resources* (3rd ed.). Dubuque, IA: Kendall/Hunt.

Reutzel, D. R., & Cooter, R. (2000). *Teaching children to read: Putting the pieces together* (3rd ed.). Columbus, OH: Merrill.

Vacca, J. A. L., Vacca, R. T., & Gove, M. K. (2000). *Reading and learning to read* (4th ed.). New York: Addison Wesley Longman.

Vacca, R. T., & Vacca, J. A. L. (2005). *Content area reading: Literacy and learning across the curriculum* (8th ed.). Boston: Allyn & Bacon.

Concept Circles

EL Beneficial when working with English learners

Strategy at a Glance: *Grade Levels All*			
When to Use	**Grouping**	**Literature Type**	**Skill Areas**
⬤ before reading	⬤ individual	◯ narrative	◯ word recognition
⬤ during reading	⬤ small group	⬤ expository	⬤ vocabulary
⬤ after reading	⬤ whole class		⬤ comprehension
	◯ center		◯ writing

Purpose

To assist in the categorization and collection of information to show the connections among concepts and their meanings from an instructional unit of study

Literature Used

Gregg Keyboarding and Personal Applications, by Alan Lloyd and others

Communicating in Spanish, by Conrad Schmitt and Protase W. Woodford

When to Use

Before, during, and/or after reading

Description of Strategy

Concept circles rely on visual representation to display whole-part connections among ideas. The parts in a circle contain concepts that all relate to each other in some way. By placing certain concepts in a circle, students are then able to determine a category (name of the circle) that all of the terms would logically belong to. Students are given the category names for each of the circles and asked to use literature they have been reading to fill in the concepts that go into each circle, or students may be given the collection of terms already in the circles and then are asked to determine the category names of the circles. In other variations, students may be given the concepts, categories, and empty concept circles and asked to determine where each would fit, or students may have to provide circles for the vocabulary and be asked to determine their own logical concepts and categories. The teacher can choose how to use this strategy based on the amount of scaffolding needed by the learners.

Procedures for Use

1. The teacher selects a unit of study containing concepts that lend themselves to logical groupings as in the *Gregg Keyboarding and Personal Applications* series for an introductory computer course.

2. *Before* students read and study the information, the teacher should preteach some of the key terms. Attention also should be drawn to important words *during* the lesson to provide multiple exposures to the vocabulary.

3. The teacher should introduce the strategy of concept circles and explain how they work, why they are helpful, and when to use them. That is, giving learners a purpose and building background are crucial components for making the activity successful.

4. *After* the information from the text has been read and discussed, the teacher asks the students to complete the concept circles. If students are not familiar with the activity, it may be helpful to demonstrate it with an example or two through modeling and/or guided practice.

5. In the example for *Gregg Keyboarding and Personal Applications* shown in Figure 18–1, students must mark out the word that does not logically fit into each circle of four terms and must determine the name of the category for the remaining three. Although these concept circles all have four terms, for other lessons there might be only three while others might have five or more per circle. The key idea is that the related terms have a logical basis for belonging to a category. Otherwise, students will misunderstand the process of classifying and collecting.

6. Instead of circles, the teacher may use concept boxes. For scaffolding in the activity for *Gregg Keyboarding and Personal Applications,* the teacher has provided a concept bank of headings or category names from which students may select correct choices to label each circle. The example from the foreign language textbook, *Communicating in Spanish,* shown in Figure 18–2, applies the principles of concept circles to names for foods. In this instance, however, baskets take the place of circles or squares. An answer key accompanies the activity. (See Figure 18–3.)

Directions: Shade the word in each concept circle that does not logically belong. On the line below each circle, write the word or phrase from the concept bank of headings to describe what the remaining words in each circle have in common.

Answer Key:

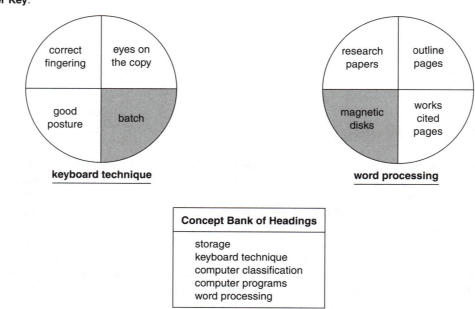

FIGURE 18–1   Example for *Gregg Keyboarding and Personal Applications*

Comprando Comestibles

Label the baskets with the store categories and sort the vocabulary words into the appropriate baskets, based on the store in which each item is sold.

La panadería
La lechería
La carnicería
La verdurería
El helado
El tocino
La leche
Las galletas
La lechuga
Las manzanas
El jamón
Las uvas
El pan
El maíz
El bistec
La mantequilla
Los limones
El pan dulce
Las zanahorias
Las fresas

La frutería

el pastel

las patatas

el queso

el pollo

FIGURE 18–2   Example for *Communicating in Spanish*

Comprando Comestibles

Label the baskets with the store categories and sort the vocabulary words into the appropriate baskets, based on the store in which each item is sold.

La panadería

el pastel
las galletas
el pan
el pan dulce

La frutería

las manzanas
las uvas
los limones
las fresas

La panadería - the bakery
La lechería - the dairy
La carnicería - the butcher shop
La verdurería - the vegetable stand
El helado - the ice cream
El tocino - the bacon
La leche - the milk
Las galletas - the cookies
La lechuga - the lettuce
Las manzanas - the apples
El jamón - the ham
Las uvas - the grapes
El pan - the bread
El maíz - the corn
El bistec - the beef
La mantequilla - the butter
Los limones - the lemons
El pan dulce - the sweet rolls
Las zanahorias - the carrots
Las fresas - the strawberries

La verdurería

las patatas
la lechuga
el maíz
las zanahorias

La lechería

el queso
la leche
el helado
la mantequilla

La carnicería

el pollo
el tocino
el jamón
el bistec

FIGURE 18–3   Answer Key for *Communicating in Spanish*

Further Reading

Gipe, J. P. (2006). *Multiple paths to literacy: Assessment and differentiated instruction for diverse learners, K–12* (6th ed.). Upper Saddle River, NJ: Merrill/Prentice Hall.

Johns, J., & Lenski, S. D. (2001). *Improving reading: Strategies and resources* (3rd ed.). Dubuque, IA: Kendall/Hunt.

Vacca, J. A. L., Vacca, R. T., & Gove, M. K. (2000). *Reading and learning to read* (4th ed.). New York: Addison Wesley Longman.

Vacca, R. T., & Vacca, J. A. L. (2005). *Content area reading: Literacy and learning across the curriculum* (8th ed.). Boston: Allyn & Bacon.

19 Analogies

Beneficial when working with English learners

Strategy at a Glance: *Grade Levels 4–8*

When to Use	Grouping	Literature Type	Skill Areas
○ before reading	● individual	● narrative	○ word recognition
○ during reading	● small group	● expository	● vocabulary
● after reading	○ whole class		● comprehension
	○ center		○ writing

Purpose

To foster critical thinking and reinforcement of key vocabulary through the comparison of relationships in two pairs of words

Literature Used

American Government: Freedom, Rights, Responsibilities, by Vivian Bernstein

When to Use

After reading

Description of Strategy

Analogies develop critical thought through a comparison of like relationships. The teacher may construct numerous types of relationships for an activity to reinforce key terms through analogies. Common types of relationships include the following, which may serve as models for the teacher when he or she creates analogies:

1. Part to whole
   a is to *alphabet* as *toe* is to *foot*

2. Cause and effect
   prosperity is to *peace* as *poverty* is to *revolution*

3. Person to situation
   King George III is to *monarchy* as *Andrew Jackson* is to *democracy*

4. Antonym
   gluttony is to *fasting* as *war* is to *peace*

5. Synonym
   mob is to *rabble* as *elite* is to *nonesuch*

6. Geography
   ocean is to *Atlantic* as *continent* is to *Australia*

7. Person or character to task, country, birthplace, and so forth.
   Perseus is to *Medusa* as *St. George* is to *dragon*

8. Time or measurement
   second is to *minute* as *hour* is to *day*

9. Symbol
   light is to *hope* as *darkness* is to *despair*

10. Characteristic or trait
    Achilles is to *courage* as *Benedict Arnold* is to *treachery*

11. Degree
    piano is to *pianissimo* as *forte* is to *fortissimo*

For younger students, the teacher may want to familiarize them first with one or two types of analogies such as part to whole or synonyms. The follow-up vocabulary reinforcement strategy would concentrate on these relationships only. For older learners, a vocabulary reinforcement activity with analogies may contain a variety of different kinds of relationships for each pair of terms. Some analogies should have contrast; others, cause and effect; still others, part to whole; and so forth. A mixture will call for greater critical thinking than an exercise that has all of the analogies with only a single relationship. If students are not familiar with analogous relationships, the teacher should build background by modeling a few examples. Once students become more comfortable with analogies, they may take key terms and write their own.

Procedures for Use

1. Chapter 14 from *American Government: Freedom, Rights, Responsibilities,* by Vivian Bernstein, discusses political parties and is rich in concepts that require multiple exposures if students are to develop word power. The teacher should carefully examine the chapter to determine which terms need emphasis in support of learning outcomes. Some of these words should be introduced *before* reading, as others are emphasized *during* reading.

2. The activity with analogies comes *after* reading and helps learners get at the deeper dimensions of the connections among concepts as students problem-solve to determine relationships.

3. The example used in Figure 19–1 contains a sample analogy that the teacher models for students to help them become familiar with the nature of analogies. Scaffolding is further provided through a multiple-choice format for each item with four choices (a, b, c, d) listed. Students could be permitted to refer to their texts for additional help if key terms are unclear or have been forgotten.

4. The activity can be completed by students individually or cooperatively. If students work in collaborative groups, they receive the added reinforcement of hearing the words, saying the words, and reading the words.

Directions: Determine the relationship between the first pair of words, and then circle the letter of the word that similarly relates the second pair of words. These words are taken from Chapter 14 of *American Government: Freedom, Rights, Responsibilities.* You may refer to your book if necessary.

Example: CAR is to GAS as SAILBOAT is to:
        a. oar   b. wind   c. water   d. waves

You should have circled the letter b. Gas powers a car, and wind powers a sailboat.

1. GAMES are to BASEBALL as ELECTIONS are to:
    a. Constitution   b. political parties   c. United States   d. the first Tuesday in November

2. FEDERALIST is to REPUBLICAN as ANTIFEDERALIST is to:
    a. Congress   b. Libertarian   c. American Independent   d. Democrat

3. THIRD PARTY is to THEODORE ROOSEVELT as AMERICAN INDEPENDENT is to:
    a. George Wallace   b. George Washington   c. Lyndon B. Johnson   d. George Bush, Sr.

4. RACE is to RUNNER as ELECTION is to:
    a. voter   b. platform   c. candidate   d. polling place

5. BOOK is to WRITER as CONSTITUTION is to:
    a. framers   b. voters   c. candidates   d. citizens

6. FOOTBALL TEAM is to FAN as CANDIDATE is to:
    a. voter   b. citizen   c. election day   d. government

7. SOUP is to GROCERIES as VOTER is to:
    a. election day   b. member of Congress   c. eighteen years old   d. registration list

8. AUTOMOBILE is to DRIVER'S LICENSE as VOTING is to:
    a. citizenship   b. president   c. platform   d. political advertisement

9. EATING is to DINING ROOM as VOTING is to:
    a. platform   b. Republicans   c. Democrats   d. polling place

10. COLD is to ICE CREAM as FREE ELECTION is to:
    a. democracy   b. volunteer worker   c. nonvoter   d. Fourth of July

Key:

1. b	6. a
2. d	7. d
3. a	8. a
4. c	9. d
5. a	10. a

FIGURE 19–1   Example for *American Government: Freedom, Rights, Responsibilities*

Further Reading

Gunning, T. (2005). *Creating literacy instruction for all students* (5th ed.). Boston: Allyn & Bacon.

Harris, A. J., & Sipay, E. R. (1990). *How to increase reading ability: A guide to developmental and remedial methods* (9th ed.). New York: Longman.

Vacca, J. A. L., Vacca, R. T., & Gove, M. K. (2000). *Reading and learning to read* (4th ed.). New York: Addison Wesley Longman.

20 Frayer Model

Beneficial when working with English learners

Strategy at a Glance: *Grade Levels All*

When to Use	Grouping	Literature Type	Skill Areas
● before reading	● individual	● narrative	○ word recognition
● during reading	● small group	● expository	● vocabulary
● after reading	● whole class		● comprehension
	○ center		○ writing

Purpose

To develop the meaning of vocabulary words through analysis of essential and nonessential properties and through examples and nonexamples

Literature Used

The Librarian who Measured the Earth, by Kathryn Lasky

When to Use

Before, during, or after reading

Description of Strategy

The Frayer Model helps students understand the deeper dimensions of a word's meaning and may be used to study a difficult vocabulary concept either *before*, *during*, or *after* reading. *Before* reading, teachers use the Frayer Model to introduce or preview a new vocabulary word. *During* reading, the strategy may serve as part of an on-the-spot mini-lesson for a difficult concept students encounter. *After* reading, the strategy may provide additional exposure to reinforce comprehension of a concept. The technique gives learners a structure, usually in the form of a four-square activity, to organize information about a word into blocks containing attributes, non-attributes, examples, and non-examples. In the center of the four squares is a circle containing the word and a definition. The purpose of the Frayer Model is to aid understanding through knowledge of what something is as well as through knowledge of what it is not.

Procedures for Use

1. On a worksheet, chart paper, overhead projector, or board, the teacher provides learners with a four-square diagram which they will use to organize information about a difficult vocabulary concept. Figure 20–1 shows one way a four square might look. Starting clockwise from the upper left box, each box is labeled as follows: essential features, non-essential features, non-examples, and examples.

2. In the center of the four-square diagram is a circle (or oval). This should be large enough so that students have room to write the word and its definition. (See Figure 20–1.) The definition may be recorded before or after students have discussed and decided upon which relevant and irrelevant features and examples go in the four boxes. The definition may be from a dictionary or in the students' own words.

3. The teacher explains the purpose of the four square and should scaffold the activity through initial modeling followed by guided practice and then independent practice for students as they complete the boxes. Students may work individually, in pairs, in small groups, or as a whole class. As learners become accustomed to the process, they can work more independently.

4. Figure 20–2 illustrates a completed four square for the concept "circumference" from Kathryn Lasky's *The Librarian Who Measured the Earth,* a picture book biography of the ancient Greek mathematician Erastothenes, who determined the circumference of the earth through logical analysis. This text might serve as helpful supplementary reading to the study of geometry in math.

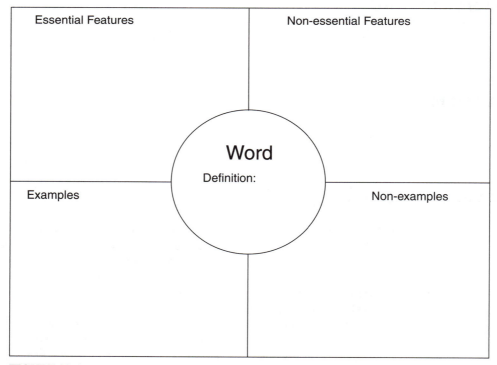

FIGURE 20–1   Example of a Four Square for the Frayer Model

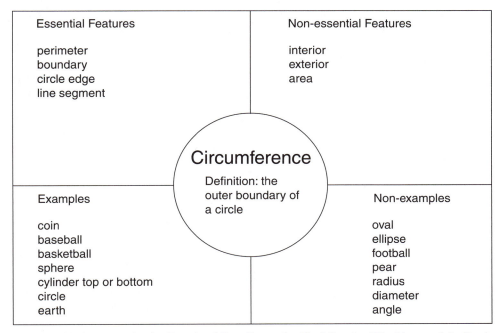

Essential Features

perimeter
boundary
circle edge
line segment

Non-essential Features

interior
exterior
area

Circumference

Definition: the
outer boundary of
a circle

Examples

coin
baseball
basketball
sphere
cylinder top or bottom
circle
earth

Non-examples

oval
ellipse
football
pear
radius
diameter
angle

FIGURE 20–2   Example of a Completed Four Square for *The Librarian Who Measured the Earth*

Further Reading

Billmeyer, R., & Barton, M. L. (2002). *Teaching reading in the content areas: If not me, then who?* (2nd ed.). Aurora, CO: Mid-Continent Research for Education and Learning.

Frayer, D. A., Frederick, W. C., & Klausmeier, H. J. (1969). *A schema for testing the level of concept mastery*. Technical Report No. 16. Madison, WI: University of Wisconsin Research and Development Center for Cognitive Learning.

Gipe, J. P. (2006). *Multiple paths to literacy: Assessment and differentiated instruction for diverse learners, K–12* (6th ed.). Upper Saddle River, NJ: Merrill/Prentice Hall.

Tierney, R. J., & Readence, J. E. (2000). *Reading strategies and practices: A compendium* (5th ed.). Boston: Allyn & Bacon.

PART IV

Comprehension Strategies

Reasons abound for reader lack of comprehension. Inattentiveness, lack of interest or motivation, insufficient background knowledge, failure to maintain schema during reading, limited vocabulary, inadequate skills necessary for particular types of comprehension tasks—all may cause problems in understanding text. As a result, students will benefit from direct instruction in comprehension.

Basal readers, school curriculum guides, and state standards provide assistance to teachers in knowing which comprehension competencies to assess and develop in learners within and across various grades. These same resources also may offer specific suggestions on how to teach comprehension. This section gives strategies helpful for growth in this aspect of the reading process for both narrative and expository text.

One useful way to think about comprehension is to consider three levels of understanding that learners may attain when encountering reading selections. At the most basic level, teachers will want learners to acquire *literal* meanings from their reading. If students are reading narrative text, examples might include recalling characters' names, where and when a story takes place, or its sequence of events. The emphasis at the literal level of reading is getting the facts from what the text *explicitly* states. Literal comprehension is important in that it forms the foundation for higher levels of understanding.

Competent readers need to have the ability to delve beneath what is literally stated or to read between the lines at an *interpretive* or *inferential* level. Here readers might determine how text is organized, find unstated relationships among ideas, predict outcomes, interpret figurative language, or summarize a passage in their own words. These kinds of abilities and others require more than the literal recall of what a writer has stated. They require learners to get information that is *implicit* in what they read.

A third type of comprehension is *application*. At this level, readers are able to make connections beyond what a text states or implies. For instance, students might make a *text-to-text* connection by comparing or contrasting a character in one story to a character in another story previously read. They might find a *text-to-world* link by observing similarities among events in history to contemporary news items. And, of course, students might discover personal or *text-to-me* connections. In reading Ezra Jack Keats' *Peter's Chair*, some readers may remember that their reactions were like Peter's when they had a new sibling at home and that they eventually made adjustments.

Comprehension is a complex part of the reading process and contains many other facets too numerous for a full accounting here. Other aspects might include *critical* thinking competencies such as distinguishing fact from opinion, recognizing propaganda, judging faulty logic, determining an author's qualifications, or evaluating the quality of resources for a research project.

An important point to make is that teachers should resist the temptation to think about various levels of comprehension and the many competencies involved as separate and discreet. All of these may overlap in a variety of ways. As with other reading abilities, like the use of word recognition and deriving vocabulary meanings, readers may simultaneously interact with text at different levels and engage in a variety of skills to create meaning. For example, expository textbooks generally state the main idea of a passage so that the level of comprehension needed is *literal*. However, if students have to combine several ideas to derive the central idea, then the level is *inferential* because the main idea may be implied or unstated. But if learners are at the same time evaluating the truthfulness, accuracy, or degree of the quality of the central idea, then they are engaged in critical reading and thinking.

Another important point is that the level of comprehension needed for reading frequently depends on the age and experience of the learner. If the teacher asks a four-year-old during a discussion of the "Three Little Pigs" whether the big bad wolf is real, the response more than likely requires critical thinking as the child attempts to distinguish between fact and fantasy. The same type of question posed to a middle school student about whether people can really fly on broomsticks will elicit literal-level answers.

An additional consideration is that teachers should take care not to isolate comprehension into a series of fragmented or *decomposed* subskills. Mastery of specific competencies like understanding the main idea, recalling significant supporting details, or determining a story problem and its solution do not necessarily indicate that learners can combine these into a meaningful whole. To use an analogy, a potential bike rider may be able to pedal, brake, balance, or guide in isolation, but all these skills and more must be coordinated to make a bike rider. So, too, in reading the creation of meaning is more than the sum of its parts.

Chaining for Time Order or for One-to-One Cause and Effect and/or Problem Solution

EL Beneficial when working with English learners

Strategy at a Glance: *Grade Levels All*

When to Use	Grouping	Literature Type	Skill Areas
○ before reading	○ individual	● narrative	○ word recognition
● during reading	● small group	● expository	● vocabulary
● after reading	● whole class		● comprehension
	○ center		● writing

Purpose

To help students understand a chronological sequence, a cause and effect series, or a problem-solution pattern of organization from a narrative or expository passage

Literature Used

If You Give a Mouse a Cookie, by Laura Numeroff

Abe Lincoln's Hat, by Martha Brenner

When to Use

During or after reading

Description of Strategy

Chaining provides a graphic representation to students to aid them in understanding chronological sequence or in comprehending how one cause may lead to one effect, which may then become a cause leading to another effect, and so on in narrative or informational text. The same idea also applies to problem-solution organizational patterns.

Procedures for Use

1. The teacher and students share a book that has sequential, or chronological, order, cause and effect relationships, or both, as is the case with *If You Give a Mouse a Cookie.*

2. The teacher and students discuss the meanings of cause and effect or of chronological order *before* reading. The discussion should apply these concepts of reading comprehension to experiences familiar to learners in order to activate their background knowledge. The teacher might say, "I was hungry" and explain that this effect caused her to get something to eat. The students then might offer some additional familiar examples of cause and effect. The discussion should also set a purpose for learners so that, when they read or listen to the text, they will know to pay attention to time sequence and/or cause and effect.

3. The teacher reads *If You Give a Mouse a Cookie* and uses a prepared chart on chronological order, cause and effect, or both. Parts of the sequence or some of the causes and effects are provided on the chart. (See the example for *If You Give a Mouse a Cookie* in Figure 21–1.) Students work with the teacher or independently to complete the chart. Some learners will need more teacher guidance than others. A picture, a word, a phrase, an entire sentence, or a combination of these may be used depending on the needs of the

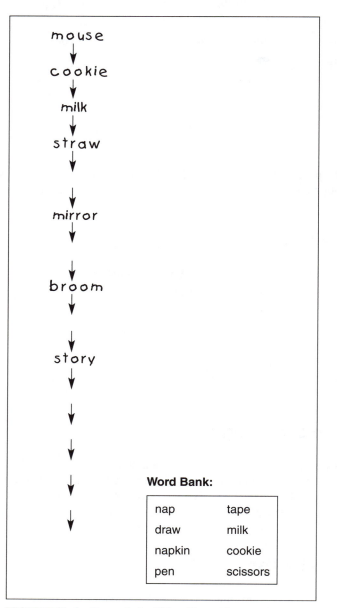

FIGURE 21–1 Example for *If You Give a Mouse a Cookie*

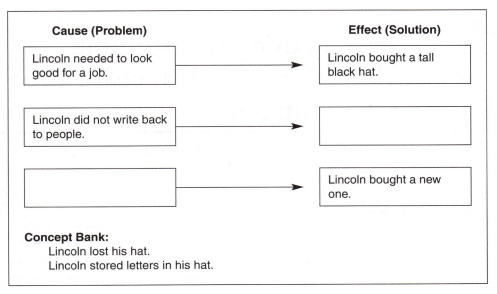

FIGURE 21–2   Example for *Abe Lincoln's Hat*

class. In the example, single words or prompts are given. The student says a sentence using the word that shows cause-effect relationships. For example, a class member might say, "Because the **mouse** was hungry, he ate a **cookie**."

4. Once the chart is completed, the teacher and students should discuss it and read it. The teacher may read it *aloud* to the students and then invite them to read *along* together, following the teacher's lead.

5. As a final step, students read the completed chart *alone*.

6. For less able learners, a concept bank of missing portions of the sequence or of causes and effects may be helpful for them to make selections to go in the chart. (This scaffolding technique is used in the example for *If You Give a Mouse a Cookie*.)

7. The example for *Abe Lincoln's Hat* in Figure 21–2 shows chains for a text in which one cause (or problem) exists for one effect (or solution). Students must determine these *during* or *after* reading. A concept bank provides additional scaffolding, if needed. Teacher modeling and guidance will be essential for some learners.

Further Reading

Cooper, J. D. (2000). *Literacy: Helping children construct meaning* (4th ed.). Boston: Houghton Mifflin.

Gunning, T. (2005). *Creating literacy instruction for all students* (5th ed.). Boston: Allyn & Bacon.

Harris, A. J., & Sipay, E. R. (1990). *How to increase reading ability: A guide to developmental and remedial methods* (9th ed.). New York: Longman.

Johns, J., & Lenski, S. D. (2001). *Improving reading: Strategies and resources* (3rd ed.). Dubuque, IA: Kendall/Hunt.

Reutzel, D. R., & Cooter, R. (2000). *Teaching children to read: Putting the pieces together* (3rd ed.). Columbus, OH: Merrill.

Tompkins, G. E. (2005). *Language arts: Patterns of practice* (6th ed.). Upper Saddle River, NJ: Merrill/Prentice Hall.

Vacca, R. T., & Vacca, J. A. L. (2005). *Content area reading: Literacy and learning across the curriculum* (8th ed.). Boston: Allyn & Bacon.

Chaining for Multiple Causes and Effects or Problem Solutions

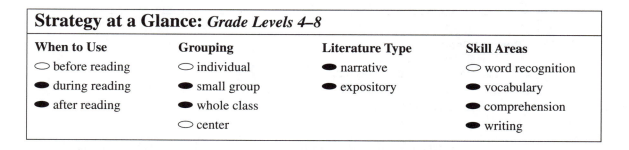 Beneficial when working with English learners

---

Strategy at a Glance: *Grade Levels 4–8*

When to Use	Grouping	Literature Type	Skill Areas
○ before reading	○ individual	● narrative	○ word recognition
● during reading	● small group	● expository	● vocabulary
● after reading	● whole class		● comprehension
	○ center		● writing

Purpose

To determine multiple causes having one effect or effects, multiple effects having one cause or causes, multiple solutions having a single problem or problems, or multiple problems having a single solution or solutions

Literature Used

Farmer Duck, by Martin Waddell

When to Use

During or after reading

Description of Strategy

Cause and effect chains can help readers understand the reason(s) for a consequence or for several consequences. The effects are recorded on a chart as a visual aid for learners to see the causes and effects (or problems and solutions) in narrative or expository text.

Procedures for Use

1. *Before* reading, the teacher prepares a cause and effect chart or problem-solution chart similar to the example for *Farmer Duck* in Figure 22–1. The teacher then decides which causes and effects to omit for students to fill in later either *during* or *after* reading. The example for *Farmer Duck* shows the completed chart. As much may be omitted or filled in as the teacher deems appropriate for the learners with whom it will be used.

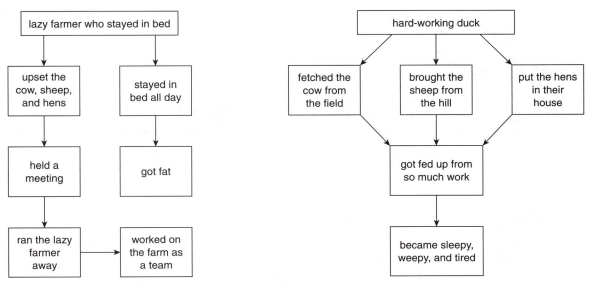

FIGURE 22–1   Example for *Farmer Duck*

2. *After* reading, the teacher models the procedure by discussing how one event results in one or several consequences, which may then become a cause or causes for other events.

3. Students will continue the procedure with teacher guidance and further modeling or thinking aloud for the remaining causes and effects.

4. A concept bank of causes and effects or problems and solutions is a helpful aid for less able learners.

Further Reading

Harris, A. J., & Sipay, E. R. (1990). *How to increase reading ability: A guide to developmental and remedial methods* (9th ed.). New York: Longman.

Reutzel, D. R., & Cooter, R. (2000). *Teaching children to read: Putting the pieces together* (3rd ed.). Columbus, OH: Merrill.

Tompkins, G. E. (2005). *Language arts: Patterns of practice* (6th ed.). Upper Saddle River, NJ: Merrill/Prentice Hall.

Vacca, R. T., & Vacca, J. A. L. (2005). *Content area reading: Literacy and learning across the curriculum* (8th ed.). Boston: Allyn & Bacon.

23 Plot-Relationship Chart

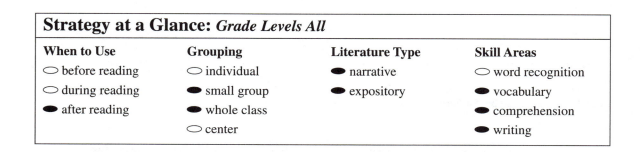

EL Beneficial when working with English learners

Purpose

To aid in the understanding and summarizing of story grammar elements, particularly main character and problem/resolution attempts in narrative material

Literature Used

"The Gambling Ghost," in *Gaelic Ghosts,* by Sorche Nic Leodhas, pages 39–46

When to Use

After reading

Description of Strategy

A plot-relationship chart is a graphic organizer consisting of four columns. Each of the columns concerns the main character, a problem that the character wants to resolve, the opposing force that gets in the way of the resolution, and how the problem is resolved. Usually the columns are labeled as follows: SOMEBODY, WANTED, BUT, and SO. SOMEBODY corresponds to the main character, or protagonist, of the story; WANTED, to the goal the protagonist wishes to accomplish or the problem to be resolved; BUT, to the antagonist, or force(s) in opposition to the main character; and SO, to how the goal is achieved or the problem is resolved. The teacher may change these column headings to better suit the capabilities of students or the age-appropriateness of the story. For instance, for older learners, the word "protagonist" may be substituted for "somebody." A plot-relationship chart also may be used to summarize or compare and contrast the plots of several different stories. This adaptation occurs by adding rows for other stories read.

Somebody	Wanted	But	So
Lad	money in order to gamble	He had taken everyone's money and did not have anyone to gamble with.	Lad gambled with a ghost who wanted to win his soul. Lad got scared, stopped gambling, got a job, and saved money.

Plot Summary Sentence(s):

_____

_____

FIGURE 23–1 Example for "The Gambling Ghost"

Procedures for Use

1. Students read independently or with teacher guidance "The Gambling Ghost" from the book *Gaelic Ghosts*.

2. The teacher and students discuss the story in terms of the chart so that students will have an idea of what the components (SOMEBODY, WANTED, BUT, SO) of the plot-relationship chart entail. (See Figure 23–1.)

3. The students fill in the chart using their own words. Teacher guidance may be necessary for some learners during this step.

4. After the chart is completed, students can summarize the plot in one or two written sentences.

5. For some learners, the chart may need to be explained *before* the story is read so that a clear purpose for reading and strategy background are established.

Further Reading

Cunningham, P., & Allington, R. (1994). *Classrooms that work*. New York: HarperCollins.

Gipe, J. P. (2006). *Multiple paths to literacy: Assessment and differentiated instruction for diverse learners, K–12* (6th ed.) Upper Saddle River, NJ: Merrill/Prentice Hall.

Harris, A. J., & Sipay, E. R. (1990). *How to increase reading ability: A guide to developmental and remedial methods* (9th ed.). New York: Longman.

Johns, J., & Lenski, S. D. (2001). *Improving reading: Strategies and resources* (3rd ed.). Dubuque, IA: Kendall/Hunt.

Norton, D. E., & Norton, S. E. (2003). *Through the eyes of a child: An introduction to children's literature* (6th ed.). Upper Saddle River, NJ: Merrill/Prentice Hall.

Tierney, R. J., & Readence, J. E. (2000). *Reading strategies and practices: A compendium* (5th ed.). Boston: Allyn & Bacon.

Tompkins, G. E. (2005). *Language arts: Patterns of practice* (6th ed.). Upper Saddle River, NJ: Merrill/Prentice Hall.

Story Pyramid

EL Beneficial when working with English learners

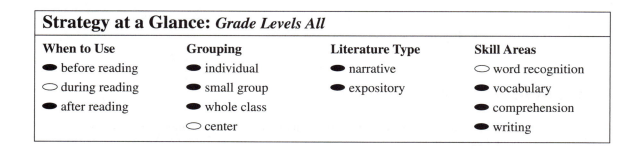

Strategy at a Glance: *Grade Levels All*

When to Use	Grouping	Literature Type	Skill Areas
● before reading	● individual	● narrative	○ word recognition
○ during reading	● small group	● expository	● vocabulary
● after reading	● whole class		● comprehension
	○ center		● writing

Purpose

To improve the ability to understand and describe such parts of story grammar in narrative writing as setting, characterization, problem-resolution, other major plot events, and theme or to aid in comprehending a key topic from expository text

Literature Used

Monster Mama, by Liz Rosenberg
The Girl Who Loved Wild Horses, by Paul Goble
Lizards and Dragons, by Lionel Bender

When to Use

After reading

Description of Strategy

The story pyramid is a comprehension activity that is often arranged in the shape of a triangle or pyramid. The first line consists of one blank, while the second line has two blanks, and so forth. Each line has a required pattern that students read and then fill in the blank(s) with information from the story to fulfill the stipulations. The teacher may record the required information, if necessary for large group work with younger children or with less able older students. The following is a sample of what each line's requirement may be:

1. Name of the main character
2. Two words describing the main character
3. Three words describing the setting
4. Four words stating the problem
5. Five words describing the first event
6. Six words describing the second event

7. Seven words describing the third event

8. Eight words stating the solution

Alterations in the requirements for each line are welcome since these may be changed to fit a particular story or the needs of different students. Some stories may need more than eight pyramid parts because these stories contain more than three major events. Another alteration is to have students write the theme or moral of the story in a complete sentence as the last line of the triangle. A further variation that might help in the facilitation of this activity is to add graphics around or to substitute them for the triangle. For example, the graphic for *Monster Mama* has students complete a triangular body of the mother in the story. (See Figure 24–1.)

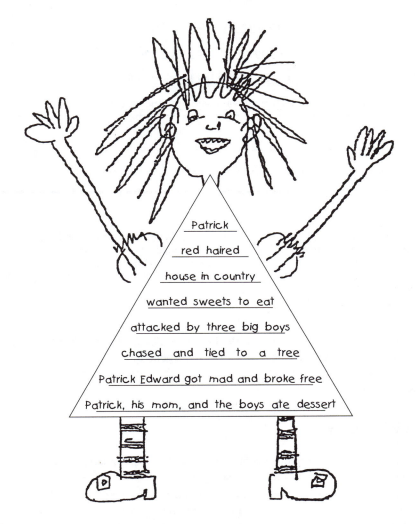

Patrick

red haired

house in country

wanted sweets to eat

attacked by three big boys

chased and tied to a tree

Patrick Edward got mad and broke free

Patrick, his mom, and the boys ate dessert

Theme or moral: _____

_____

Story Pyramid

1. Name of the main character
2. Two words describing the main character
3. Three words describing the setting
4. Four words stating the problem
5. Five words describing the first event
6. Six words describing the second event
7. Seven words describing the third event
8. Eight words stating the solution
9. (*Optional*) A sentence stating the theme or moral of the story

FIGURE 24–1   Example for *Monster Mama*

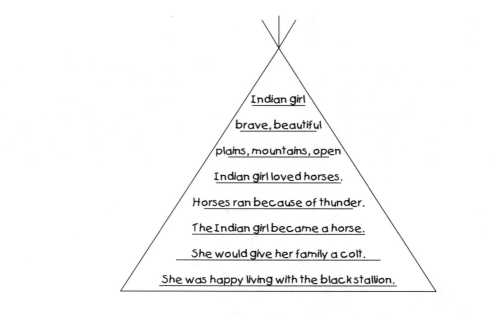

Theme or moral: _____

_____

_____

Story Pyramid

1. Name of the main character
2. Two words describing the main character
3. Three words describing the setting
4. Four words stating the problem
5. Five words describing the first event

6. Six words describing the second event
7. Seven words describing the third event
8. Eight words stating the solution
9. (*Optional*) A sentence stating the theme or moral of the story

FIGURE 24–2   Example for *The Girl Who Loved Wild Horses*

The graphic for a story pyramid of Paul Goble's *The Girl Who Loved Wild Horses* is done in the shape of a teepee since the book is about a legend of the Plains Indians. (See Figure 24–2.) The strategy not only fosters understanding of the story elements but also promotes competence in summarizing text.

Procedures for Use

1. Any narrative or expository text may be used, whether poetry or prose depending on how the teacher structures students' responses.

2. Based on the students' needs, the teacher decides the reading mode; for *Monster Mama* and *The Girl Who Loved Wild Horses,* the selected mode is read *aloud, along,* and *alone* so as to give the necessary scaffolding for learners to aid in sight word recognition through repeated readings. This procedure facilitates automaticity in pronouncing words.

3. Students listen carefully as the teacher reads *aloud*.

4. Students read the text *along* with the teacher and then, as a final step, read *alone*.

5. The teacher describes and explains the story pyramid and sets the purpose for using it.

6. If readers have not previously worked with story pyramids, the teacher may want to guide them in arriving at the answers. For example, the first line of the pyramid for *Monster Mama* would be "Patrick," the name of the little boy in the story.

7. The students complete the pyramid by filling in the blanks. The teacher provides instructional guidance as necessary. The information on the pyramid may be used to model a retelling of the story.

Alternate Idea

The teacher or student(s) may record responses on cardboard boxes with one word written on each box for a total of twenty-one boxes for a three-dimensional pyramid. (Instead of writing on the boxes, students may record responses on self adhesive notes to attach to the boxes later.) Thus, the answer for question one is one word recorded on one box, while the answer for question two is two words recorded on two boxes. This procedure continues through question six, for which six words are written on six boxes. Once all the questions are answered, students should stack their boxes in the reverse order in which the questions were asked. The six boxes for question six become the base, those for question five the next layer, those for question four the next, and so on. This process continues until the pyramid is built with the last box for question one being the apex. (See Figure 24–3.) Kinesthetic or tactile learners will especially benefit from this adaptation.

A good way to familiarize learners not acquainted with a three-dimensional text pyramid is to have them build a pyramid about themselves before making one based on a reading passage. The following are hypothetical questions to use for an initial pyramid:

1. What is your name?
2. What are two words that describe you?
3. What are three words describing where you live?
4. Who are four of your friends?
5. What are five features that all of them have that make you like them?
6. What are six of the favorite things you like to do with your friends (foods to eat, places to go, and so on)?

As item six shows, the teacher may alter the questions as necessary.

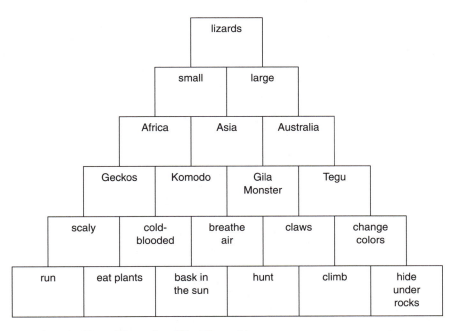

Questions for Three-Dimensional Text Pyramid

1. What is the main topic or subject of the reading passage? (The answer may be one word or several).
2. What are two words that describe the main topic in question one?
3. Where are three continents where the main topic in question one is found?
4. What are four examples of the main topic in question one?
5. What are five characteristics that may describe the main topic in question one or the four examples in question four?
6. What are six words or phrases that may describe what the four examples in question four do?

FIGURE 24–3 Example of a Three-Dimensional Text Pyramid Using Expository Text.

Further Reading

Harris, A. J., & Sipay, E. R. (1990). *How to increase reading ability: A guide to developmental and remedial methods* (9th ed.). New York: Longman.

Johns, J., & Lenski, S. D. (2001). *Improving reading: Strategies and resources* (3rd ed.). Dubuque, IA: Kendall/Hunt.

Norton, D. E., & Norton, S. E. (2003). *Through the eyes of a child: An introduction to children's literature* (6th ed.). Upper Saddle River, NJ: Merrill/Prentice Hall.

Tierney, R. J., & Readence, J. E. (2000). *Reading strategies and practices: A compendium* (5th ed.). Boston: Allyn & Bacon.

Tompkins, G. E. (2005). *Language arts: Patterns of practice* (6th ed.). Upper Saddle River, NJ: Merrill/Prentice Hall.

Picture Walk or Text Walk

EL Beneficial when working with English learners

Strategy at a Glance: *Grade Levels All*			
When to Use	**Grouping**	**Literature Type**	**Skill Areas**
● before reading	○ individual	● narrative	○ word recognition
○ during reading	● small group	● expository	● vocabulary
○ after reading	● whole class		● comprehension
	○ center		○ writing

Purpose

To improve comprehension by activating the reader's background of experience or by developing additional knowledge about the content, organization, and vocabulary of narrative or expository text

Literature Used

The Story of Ferdinand, by Munro Leaf

When to Use

Before reading

Description of Strategy

Before reading occurs, the teacher previews and discusses the passage and asks questions about any illustrations, photographs, charts, or other graphics, whether the text is narrative or expository. In this way, students are provided with an overview of important ideas, organizational structure, and key vocabulary words. Before doing the picture or text walk, the teacher should read through the passage that will be used and note important concepts and vocabulary to emphasize. During this phase, the teacher should also jot down any questions that will activate a reader's background knowledge and develop an understanding of the reading material. A good idea is to include both efferent and aesthetic questions or comments during the picture or text walk. Efferent questions or comments will draw attention to important content ideas or to literacy competencies relevant in the passage such as main ideas, details, or significant vocabulary words, whereas aesthetic questions or comments will engage students on a personal level so that motivation for reading is likely increased. Usually, the term "picture walk" is preferred when the strategy is used for narrative text in picture books. The term "text walk" is used when the passage is from content-area materials or expository writing. In many instances, the teacher will want to do a picture or text walk on only a portion of the reading material, particularly when storybooks or narrative texts have unusual happenings or surprise endings that should not be revealed beforehand to learners.

Procedures for Use

1. The teacher should read *The Story of Ferdinand* ahead of time to determine the key components of the storyline and to decide which illustrations best reflect those ideas in order to preview and discuss them with students.

2. The teacher may begin the picture walk by stating the title and showing students the cover of the book, featuring Ferdinand the Bull. Efferent questions or prompts may be asked such as "What is Ferdinand doing? Where is he standing? What does it look like he is smelling?" The white daisies may be emphasized since Ferdinand's favorite activity is to sit quietly under the cork tree and smell the flowers.

3. The teacher may want to discuss the inside cover of the book to show students how the people of Madrid mistakenly think that Ferdinand is a fierce bull. The Spanish phrase "EL TORO FEROZ FERDINANDO" on the advertisement for the bullfight may be translated for students to point out the contrast between the people's perception of Ferdinand as a large, fierce bull and his true gentle nature. Some examples of aesthetic questions might include "Have you ever seen a bull? Did you think it looked ferocious? Do you think Ferdinand looks ferocious in the poster on the inside front cover? Would you want to fight a bull that looked like this picture of Ferdinand? How about here in the picture showing Ferdinand as a young bull sitting under the cork tree where he watches the other young bulls run and butt their heads together?"

4. To aid with understanding difficult vocabulary words, the teacher may want to preview some of the illustrations of the participants in the bullfight in Madrid by emphasizing pictures of the banderilleros, the picadores, and the matador.

5. In a picture walk with this text, it is likely that the teacher will not want to showcase the illustrations and story in the last few pages since Ferdinand surprises the bullfighters and the people in the arena by sitting down and refusing to fight because he smells flowers in the hair of the lovely ladies in attendance. However, the teacher may ask students to make predictions about this portion of the plot so that, when the story is read later, the students may verify their hypotheses.

6. Students can now read the story in whatever mode is appropriate, whether shared, guided, cooperative, or independent. Alternatively, the teacher may read the story aloud as students listen.

Further Reading

Cooper, J. D. (2000). *Literacy: Helping children construct meaning* (4th ed.). Boston: Houghton Mifflin.

Gunning, T. (2005). *Creating literacy instruction for all students* (5th ed.). Boston: Allyn & Bacon.

Johns, J., & Lenski, S. D. (2001). *Improving reading: Strategies and resources* (3rd ed.). Dubuque, IA: Kendall/Hunt.

Reutzel, D. R., & Cooter, R. (2000). *Teaching children to read: Putting the pieces together* (3rd ed.). Columbus, OH: Merrill.

Tompkins, G. E. (2005). *Language arts: Patterns of practice* (6th ed.). Upper Saddle River, NJ: Merrill/Prentice Hall.

Readers' Theater

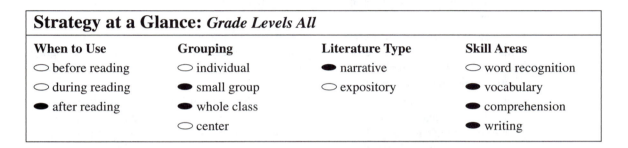

Strategy at a Glance: *Grade Levels All*

When to Use	Grouping	Literature Type	Skill Areas
○ before reading	○ individual	● narrative	○ word recognition
○ during reading	● small group	○ expository	● vocabulary
● after reading	● whole class		● comprehension
	○ center		● writing

Purpose

To enhance listening, speaking, reading, and writing through creative interpretations of narrative text

Literature Used

"The Story of the Three Little Pigs," from Joseph Jacobs' *English Fairy Tales*

When to Use

After reading

Description of Strategy

Readers' theater is a strategy that fosters comprehension through creative interpretations of narratives by engaging students in role-playing stories, poems, or songs. Although the strategy focuses on the oral aspect of the language arts by allowing students to bring the characters to life through their voices, other language arts such as listening and reading are also integrated. Once learners are accustomed to the technique of readers' theater, they may create scripts and thereby develop facility with writing. When presenting readers' theater, students do not memorize lines; instead, as the name says, they *read* from a script after they have had time to practice good oral interpretation skills.

Procedures for Use

1. *After* the teacher and students have studied a narrative text, whether picture book, novel, poem, or song, the teacher may decide that the text is appropriate for readers' theater as an enrichment activity that develops literary appreciation as well as language arts

competencies. The key consideration is that the passage have enough dialogue for division into different character roles for students to read.

2. The teacher and students divide the text into parts. Students should have a copy of the passage to mark. More advanced students may divide the text on their own for presentation.

3. With the teacher's assistance, students identify and list all the characters. Their speaking parts are then marked and narrative tags such as "he said" or "she said" are omitted, leaving only the dialogue. Students are assigned these parts to read. A single character may have more than one reader. In fact, two or more students can simultaneously read one character's dialogue. The point is that all members of the class participate either as characters or narrators. In point of fact, essential narrative sections may be retained for oral reading by one narrator, by several separate narrators taking turns, or by a group of narrators functioning as a chorus.

4. Theatrical interpolations may be added such as a scream, a whistle, or an animal sound like a dog's bark. In "The Story of the Three Little Pigs," a theatrical interpolation might be the knocking by the wolf on the door of one of the pigs. A student can make this sound effect when the script requires it.

5. As steps 3 and 4 indicate, an essential key to readers' theater is that each student is involved. No one is left out. As each student chooses or is assigned to a role, these are marked on the passage with **N** for narrator or with a character's name. Sometimes different colored pens for each part work well. For interpolations, students make notes as to the time they are to create a sound effect.

6. The teacher should allow students time to prepare and rehearse the play before it is presented so that they may hone good oral interpretation skills with literature.

7. Readers' theater works also well for small collaborative groups within a class to present different stories studied. In a unit on folklore, one group might present "The Story of the Three Little Pigs"; another, "Henny Penny"; and another, "Goldilocks and the Three Bears." As students prepare and rehearse their stories, they develop skills in cooperative problem solving.

Further Reading

Cooper, J. D. (2000). *Literacy: Helping children construct meaning* (4th ed.). Boston: Houghton Mifflin.

Gunning, T. (2005). *Creating literacy instruction for all students* (5th ed.). Boston: Allyn & Bacon.

Johns, J., & Lenski, S. D. (2001). *Improving reading: Strategies and resources* (3rd ed.). Dubuque, IA: Kendall/Hunt.

Reutzel, D. R., & Cooter, R. (2000). *Teaching children to read: Putting the pieces together* (3rd ed.). Columbus, OH: Merrill.

Ruddell, R. B., & Ruddell, M. R. (1995). *Teaching children to read and write: Becoming an influential teacher*. Boston: Allyn & Bacon.

Tierney, R. J., & Readence, J. E. (2000). *Reading strategies and practices: A compendium* (5th ed.). Boston: Allyn & Bacon.

Tompkins, G. E. (2005). *Language arts: patterns of practice* (6th ed.). Upper Saddle River, NJ: Merrill/Prentice Hall.

Wood, K. D., & Dickinson, T. S. (Eds.). (2000). *Promoting literacy in grades 4–9: A handbook for teachers and administrators*. Boston: Allyn & Bacon.

KWL

EL Beneficial when working with English learners

Strategy at a Glance: *Grade Levels All*

When to Use	Grouping	Literature Type	Skill Areas
● before reading	○ individual	○ narrative	○ word recognition
● during reading	● small group	● expository	● vocabulary
● after reading	● whole class		● comprehension
	● center		● writing

Purpose

To engage students in creating meaning from text as they develop background knowledge, take ownership for learning, and organize information for retrieval

Literature Used

The Art of Ancient Egypt Under the Pharaohs, by Shirley Glubok

When to Use

Before, during, and after reading

Description of Strategy

In the acronym **KWL**, **K** stands for the "knowledge" already possessed by learners about a topic *before* reading begins; **W** represents "what" they want to learn *during* reading; and **L** stands for the information "learned" *after* reading or what may still need to be learned. Through the KWL strategy, students build and activate prior knowledge through brainstorming, asking questions about areas to investigate further, summarizing what they have learned, and determining what they need to extend their learning. This process occurs through teacher guidance in the form of a KWL chart.

Procedures for Use

1. The teacher introduces a new topic of study as well as the process of the KWL strategy. In this case, the topic is the art of ancient Egypt for a class of middle school students. *Before* reading, the teacher explains the parts of KWL and each section of the chart. (See the

K—What I Know	W—What I Want to Know	L—What I Learned and Still Need to Learn

Categories of Information I Expect to Use

A.

B.

C.

D.

E.

F.

G.

FIGURE 27–1   Example of a KWL Chart

example of a KWL chart in Figure 27–1.) The KWL chart for ancient Egyptian art contains all sections of a typical KWL graphic organizer except for the adaptation of pyramids representing "What I know" for **K,** "What I want to know" for **W,** and "What I learned and still need to learn" for **L.** Students record questions for the **K** and **W** columns on the pyramids, for the pyramids below the **L** columns, students record information learned. Pyramids may be added to each column as needed. (See the example for *The Art of Ancient Egypt Under the Pharaohs* in Figure 27–2.)

2. The teacher asks students to identify what they already know about ancient Egyptian art. They may record these responses on individual sheets, or they may give answers that the teacher writes on a transparency or chart paper for the entire class to see. Responses are recorded on the pyramids under the pharaoh head labeled "What I *know*" and may be recorded in abbreviated form. The teacher's role in this stage is to facilitate students' recall of what they think they know, not to determine the rightness or wrongness of the information. Some examples of student prior knowledge are as follows:

    a. They had lots of statues made out of stone.

    b. They had a Sphinx.

    c. They had beautiful gems and jewels (jewelry).

    d. They used natural resources.

    e. They had great architects. Things were built for the weather and lasted a long time.

    f. The pictures they painted of people were very flat and had their heads turned sideways.

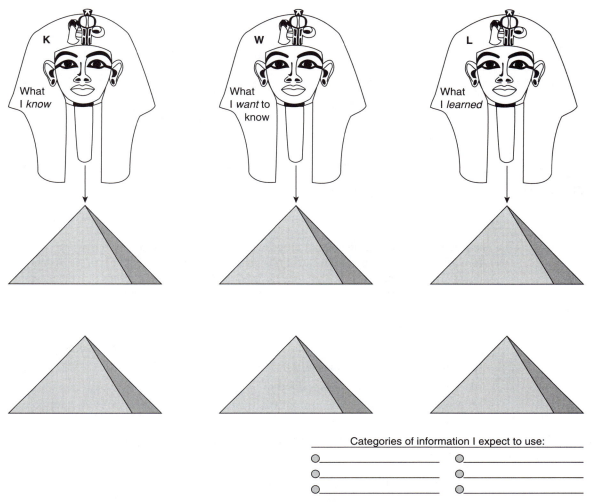

FIGURE 27–2 Example for *The Art of Ancient Egypt Under the Pharaohs*

3. With teacher guidance, students generate questions concerning information they want to know about ancient Egyptian art. The teacher may need to model this stage of the process to get students started. Questions are recorded in the "What I *want* to know" column. Below are a few of these:

   a. Why did they wrap mummies?

   b. Why did they have a gold coffin to put mummies in?

   c. What's a pyramid? Are there houses or tombs in there? Is a tomb where you put a mummy?

   d. Why did they use so much makeup and make their faces look so weird?

   e. Do we really know enough about Egypt to ask questions?

4. The teacher should aid students in making connections between what they know already and questions they want answered by the reading. As this information is discussed, students should try to group ideas into categories. These should be listed on the KWL chart if students anticipate that the text will elaborate on them further. Based on prior knowledge and questions, some potential categories of information from *The Art of Ancient Egypt Under the Pharaohs* might be **statues, paintings, pyramids, jewelry**, and **burial customs**. The teacher and students may generate additional categories *during* reading in the next step.

FIGURE 27–3   Example of a Thinking Tree for *The Art of Ancient Egypt Under the Pharaohs*

5. The teacher directs students to read for answers to questions asked previously or to list information related to any of the categories generated. This phase is the **L** of the KWL process. Students may record what they have learned as they read, or they and the teacher may record their newfound knowledge once the reading is completed as part of class discussion. The teacher might use such prompts to foment discussion as:

   a. What have we learned from our reading?

   b. What came to mind that you still have questions about as you were reading?

   c. What were some new questions that came up as you read?

   d. Where can we write our new questions on the chart?

   e. Does any of the information from your reading fit into the categories we have on our chart—for example, *pyramids*?

   f. Do we want to add any new categories of information to our chart—for example, *burial symbols?*

6. Although not required, a final step might be for the teacher and students to create a graphic organizer to show main idea–detail relationships among information learned during the process of completing a **KWL**. For *The Art of Ancient Egypt Under the Pharaohs*, students categorized, in the form of a thinking tree, information learned under the headings of two-dimensional and three-dimensional art. This activity provided a way for them to summarize information visually so that they would remember it better. (See the example of the thinking tree for ancient Egyptian art in Figure 27–3.)

Further Reading

Cooper, J. D. (2000). *Literacy: Helping children construct meaning* (4th ed.). Boston: Houghton Mifflin.

Cooter, R. B., Jr., & Flynt, E. S. (1996). *Teaching reading in the content areas: Developing content literacy for all students*. Englewood Cliffs, NJ: Prentice Hall.

Cunningham, P. M., Moore, S. A., Cunningham, J. W., & Moore, D. W. (1995). *Reading and writing in elementary classrooms: Strategies and observations* (3rd ed.). White Plains, NY: Longman.

Gipe, J. P. (2006). *Multiple paths to literacy: Assessment and differentiated instruction for diverse learners, K–12* (6th ed.). Upper Saddle River, NJ: Merrill/Prentice Hall.

Graves, M., Juel, C., & Graves, B. (1998). *Teaching reading in the 21st century*. Needham Heights, MA: Allyn & Bacon.

Gunning, T. (2005). *Creating literacy instruction for all students* (5th ed.). Boston: Allyn & Bacon.

Johns, J., & Lenski, S. D. (2001). *Improving reading: Strategies and resources* (3rd ed.). Dubuque, IA: Kendall/Hunt.

Reutzel, D. R., & Cooter, R. (2000). *Teaching children to read: Putting the pieces together* (3rd ed.). Columbus, OH: Merrill.

Ruddell, R. B., & Ruddell, M. R. (1995). *Teaching children to read and write: Becoming an influential teacher*. Boston: Allyn & Bacon.

Vacca, R. T., & Vacca, J. A. L. (2005). *Content area reading: Literacy and learning across the curriculum* (8th ed.). Boston: Allyn & Bacon.

Wood, K. D., & Dickinson, T. S. (Eds.). (2000). *Promoting literacy in grades 4–9: A handbook for teachers and administrators*. Boston: Allyn & Bacon.

SQ3R

EL Beneficial when working with English learners

Strategy at a Glance: *Grade Levels 4–8*

When to Use	Grouping	Literature Type	Skill Areas
● before reading	● individual	○ narrative	○ word recognition
● during reading	○ small group	● expository	● vocabulary
● after reading	● whole class		● comprehension
	○ center		● writing

Purpose

To help organize, elaborate, rehearse, and remember important information from text

Literature Used

HBJ Science, by Elizabeth K. Cooper and others

When to Use

Before, during, and after reading

Description of Strategy

With this procedure, students learn how to study text and retain important information through *surveying, questioning, reading, reciting,* and *reviewing*. The acronym SQ3R stands for these five components.

Procedures for Use

1. Students will be studying the first chapter, "On a Spaceship to the Planets," from the third-grade textbook, *HBJ Science*. As part of the *before* reading survey of the chapter, they should read the introduction, summary, captions under illustrations and other visuals, key vocabulary words, and section headings within the chapter. In short, students should preview anything in the passage that will build background knowledge when they begin the reading phase of SQ3R.

2. *Before* reading, as students *survey* textual information, they should ask *questions*. For students unfamiliar with the process of SQ3R, the teacher should model how the two steps work together. For this passage, the teacher demonstrates how to turn section headings into questions so that readers must actively look for answers. For instance, the heading "First Stop—Mercury" could become "Where is Mercury?" or "What is Mercury like?" The same questioning process may be demonstrated with key vocabulary in boldface or with captions under any graphics in the chapter. Students should record questions on a piece of paper.

3. *During* reading, the teacher instructs students to *read* silently to find answers to their questions. (This step is the first of the three Rs in SQ3R.) It is probably best, when students are first using SQ3R, to have them read one section at a time rather than the whole chapter. They can ask questions and find answers to longer text passages as they gradually become more independent with the process. Initially, however, there may be a great need for guided practice before independence is achieved.

4. *After* students complete their reading of a section, they try to answer (*recite*) their pre-reading question(s). The answer to "Where is Mercury?" might be "Mercury is the closest planet to the sun." The answer to "What is Mercury like?" might be "It is the hottest planet. It is so hot no plants or animals live there." Students should try to answer the questions without looking back at the text. If they can successfully answer questions once they have read the section, they are ready to write their responses.

5. If students are unable to answer a question, they should reread the section before going to the next one. This final step is the third **R** of the SQ3R—namely, the *review* portion of the process.

6. When students have completed one section of the chapter, they repeat the same procedure for SQ3R with the next section. The teacher may allow them to become more independent with each subsequent section.

7. Once SQ3R has been used for all of the first chapter, students should put away their texts and cover their notes. As a final grand review, they ask themselves the survey questions that they have already answered to determine if they can still recall vital information for each one. If they cannot, then further reading and reviewing of the text will need to occur.

8. The teacher should realize that the procedure may take a while for students to master and may require extensive practice and guidance. However, the process is well worth teaching to students in the elementary grades and beyond as a way to help them monitor and take ownership for their own learning.

Further Reading

Gunning, T. (2005). *Creating literacy instruction for all students* (5th ed.). Boston: Allyn & Bacon.

Harris, A. J., & Sipay, E. R. (1990). *How to increase reading ability: A guide to developmental and remedial methods* (9th ed.). New York: Longman.

Johns, J., & Lenski, S. D. (2001). *Improving reading: Strategies and resources* (3rd ed.). Dubuque, IA: Kendall/Hunt.

Reutzel, D. R., & Cooter, R. (2000). *Teaching children to read: Putting the pieces together* (3rd ed.). Columbus, OH: Merrill.

Robinson, F. (1946). *Effective study*. New York: HarperCollins.

Taylor, B., Harris, L. A., Pearson, P. D., & Garcia, G. (1995). *Reading difficulties: Instruction and assessment* (2nd ed.). New York: McGraw-Hill.

Tierney, R. J., & Readence, J. E. (2000). *Reading strategies and practices: A compendium* (5th ed.). Boston: Allyn & Bacon.

Tompkins, G. E. (2005). *Language arts: Patterns of practice* (6th ed.). Upper Saddle River, NJ: Merrill/Prentice Hall.

29 Mapping with Guided Reading Procedure (GRP)

EL Beneficial when working with English learners

Strategy at a Glance: *Grade Levels 4–8*			
When to Use	**Grouping**	**Literature Type**	**Skill Areas**
● before reading	○ individual	● narrative	○ word recognition
● during reading	● small group	● expository	● vocabulary
● after reading	● whole class		● comprehension
	○ center		● writing

Purpose

To organize text so that students comprehend the interrelationships among ideas presented

Literature Used

"The Indians of the Southwest Develop an Advanced Society," from *Our Country: People in Time and Place,* by Herbert J. Bass

When to Use

Before, during, and/or after reading

Description of Strategy

Mapping is an organizational technique through which students visually represent connections among main ideas and supporting details from text. The main idea is placed in the center of the map from which supporting details branch. These in turn may become main ideas for other supporting details as the map connects general concepts to information that is ever more specific. Mapping improves comprehension at any stage of the reading process. If the teacher provides students a map *before* reading, it gives them an overview of information from a passage. *During* or *after* reading, they may add to the map new information that they have learned. As maps evolve *during* reading, they remind students how ideas develop and fit together from text. Completed maps *after* reading provide a summary and review to reinforce content.

Procedures for Use

1. The teacher introduces the topic of study, "The Indians of the Southwest Develop an Advanced Society," from *Our Country: People in Time and Place,* a text intended for fifth

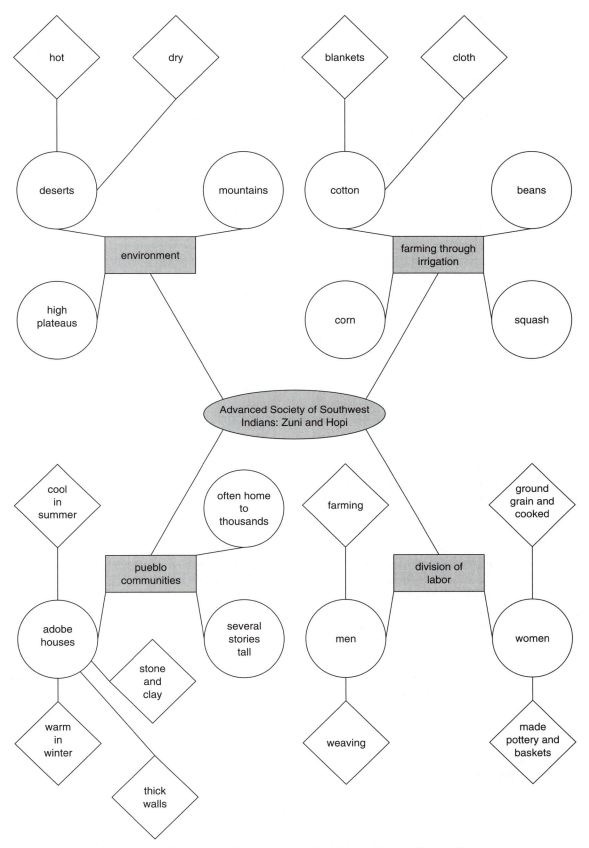

FIGURE 29–1 Example for "The Indians of the Southwest Develop an Advanced Society"

grade. A version of this topic is written in the oval (or any preferred shape) in the center of the map, whether on the chalkboard, chart paper, overhead projector, or individual student sheets. As the main idea of the passage, it is the superordinate concept from which other ideas stem. (See the example for "The Indians of the Southwest Develop an Advanced Society" in Figure 29–1.)

2. At this point, the teacher may want to encourage students to ask questions that require them to hypothesize about the topic. One prompt might be "What do you think were some characteristics of Southwest Indian society?" Another might be "Who were the Indians of the Southwest and what were their lives like?" From these questions, students can make predictions about how these Indians built shelters, grew food, and worked. Students can also hypothesize about the natural environment of these people. Such predictions will stir curiosity and spur students to read the passage in an active search for information. For less capable learners, the teacher may read the passage aloud and ask them to listen attentively.

3. Students read (or listen) to gather details about how Southwest Indians lived. Students try to recall as many details as they can remember as the teacher or another recorder lists these for students to see. If any information is incorrect, the teacher directs students in purposeful rereading or has them listen again as portions are read aloud to clear up misconceptions. Together, the teacher and students modify the list until they are satisfied about its accuracy based on the text.

4. The teacher directs students to examine the list and to group ideas into categories by looking for common features. From the list, details fall into four major headings about Southwest Indians: environment, farming through irrigation, pueblo communities, and division of labor. These headings are major subordinate details for the overall topic and are coordinate with each other. To indicate this relationship, the teacher or students write these details in shapes that branch off from the main idea—in this case, boxes. (See Figure 29–1.)

5. The teacher and students now add details from the list that branch off from the appropriate supporting details. For instance, three details that go with the box "environment" are "deserts," "mountains," and "high plateaus." These are recorded in a different shape, here circles, again to show further subordination of details. The same procedure occurs for details that go with the boxed headings "farming through irrigation," "pueblo communities," and "division of labor."

6. If categorization is a major goal of the guided reading, *after* reading (or listening) students may tell all the facts they remember about Southwest Indians while the teacher records these on chart paper. These details are then cut apart, and students group them into categories and name the categories. From the categories and details, students create their own visual representation of a map with different shapes to indicate superordinate, coordinate, and subordinate ideas. (This process greatly resembles open sorts, described in the section on vocabulary, pages 61–64.)

7. After the map is complete, teachers may want to check for student understanding of the guided reading by giving a short quiz. Another follow-up activity might be to have learners take the information from the map and construct paragraphs with main ideas and supporting details, thus further developing competence in summarizing through writing.

Further Reading

Cooter, R. B., Jr., & Flynt, E. S. (1996). *Teaching reading in the content areas: Developing content literacy for all students*. Englewood Cliffs, NJ: Prentice Hall.

Vacca, R. T., & Vacca, J. A. L. (2005). *Content area reading: Literacy and learning across the curriculum* (8th ed.). Boston: Allyn & Bacon.

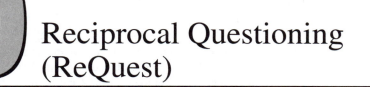

Reciprocal Questioning (ReQuest)

EL Beneficial when working with English learners

Strategy at a Glance: *Grade Levels All*

When to Use	Grouping	Literature Type	Skill Areas
○ before reading	● individual	● narrative	○ word recognition
● during reading	● small group	● expository	● vocabulary
● after reading	● whole class		● comprehension
	○ center		○ writing

Purpose

To promote comprehension through questions that the teacher and students take turns in asking one another

Literature Used

The Jolly Mon, by Jimmy Buffett and Savannah Jane Buffett

When to Use

During and after reading

Description of Strategy

ReQuest, or reciprocal questioning, develops comprehension because readers select information, ask questions about it, predict outcomes, and then confirm or reject their predictions. This reading-questioning procedure gives students the opportunity to improve their understanding of what they have read by letting them come up with questions to ask the teacher that resemble those they think the teacher might ask them. The strategy will work with one student or with larger groups. The teacher first models questions to students to guide them in getting meaning and to help them come up with thought-provoking questions that will allow critical thinking. Students are encouraged to reflect on what they have heard and read and to organize their reflections.

The strategy starts with the teacher stating the purpose. The teacher and students then read a sentence or group of sentences (no longer than a paragraph) silently. Students who do not comprehend well may need to read very short pieces of text. For nonreaders, the teacher may elect to read aloud only one or two sentences to which students listen before they ask the teacher questions. The teacher and students take turns asking questions. All questions asked deserve to be answered as fully and honestly as possible. If questions are unclear, requests for rephrasing are allowed. The responder can refer to the text to justify an answer but should have the book closed during listening and answering.

The teacher should actively attempt to model good questioning behavior. The teacher may have to stop, when questions are beyond the literal level, and may have to point out explicitly to learners what makes a question of a higher level than simple recall of information. This process continues until enough information has been gained for readers to make predictions about the remainder of the assignment. When the reading is completed, the teacher and students discuss whether the predictions were confirmed by the text. Purposeful rereading for clarification may be necessary.

Procedures for Use

1. The passage should have a reading level commensurate with that of the students. If not, the teacher may read orally to them. The passage should also contain enough information so that the students and the teacher can ask a number of questions about it.

2. *Before* reading, the teacher explains the ReQuest procedure and its purpose to students. "This lesson will help you understand better what we will read today. We will silently read our story, *The Jolly Mon*, by Jimmy Buffett and Savannah Jane Buffett. *After* we read parts of the story, we will take turns asking each other questions about it. You get to ask me questions first, and then I'll ask you some questions. When you ask questions, try to ask them the way I would ask them as your teacher. Try to make me think hard. You may ask as many questions as you like. We will keep our books closed as we ask each other questions."

3. At this point, the teacher may want to engage students in a brief survey of the book or do a short picture walk. (See pages 91–92.) Such a preview will motivate reader interest and will activate or build background knowledge. The teacher might read the title, analyze with students any illustrations that are part of the introduction, and get predictions on what the selection is about. The teacher might say "The cover of *The Jolly Mon* shows a young black man with long braids standing on a boat looking out to the green-blue sea. Also, the title uses the word 'Mon' instead of 'Man.' The author is a well-known singer/songwriter of Caribbean-style songs. All of these clues indicate that the story is about a young man from the Caribbean." If a map is available, the teacher may show the location of the setting.

4. The teacher instructs students to read the first significant segment of text silently and directs them to think of questions to ask. Students may make up as many questions as they want. The teacher silently reads the selection also.

5. All close their books. If needed, questions may be restated or clarified. Answers may be checked by looking back at the text. The story states, "Had it not been for the threat of the pirates, Bananaland would have been the most peaceful place on earth." A higher-order question a student might ask about this sentence is "Why do you think the island was called Bananaland?"

6. After students have asked questions, the teacher asks and models higher-level questioning. A question the teacher might ask is "What was dangerous about Bananaland and what does that imply might happen later in the story?" As the reading and questioning progresses, the teacher can explain difficult vocabulary or concepts.

7. The questioning continues after each passage is read until enough information has been assembled so that a purpose is set for reading the rest of the text without reciprocal questioning. A purpose question that requires prediction is: "What do you think will be the outcome of the story? Why?"

8. After the rest of the story has been read silently, the purpose question and any other questions about the story are discussed as students verify their predictions.

Further Reading

Cooter, R. B., Jr., & Flynt, E. S. (1996). *Teaching reading in the content areas: Developing content literacy for all students*. Englewood Cliffs, NJ: Prentice Hall.

Graves, M., Juel, C., & Graves, B. (1998). *Teaching reading in the 21st century*. Needham Heights, MA: Allyn & Bacon.

Gunning, T. (2005). *Creating literacy instruction for all students* (5th ed.). Boston: Allyn & Bacon.

Manzo, A. V. (1969). The ReQuest procedure. *Journal of Reading*, *11*, 123–126.

Reutzel, D. R., & Cooter, R. (2000). *Teaching children to read: Putting the pieces together* (3rd ed.). Columbus, OH: Merrill.

Ruddell, R. B., & Ruddell, M. R. (1995). *Teaching children to read and write: Becoming an influential teacher*. Boston: Allyn & Bacon.

Taylor, B., Harris, L. A., Pearson, P. D., & Garcia, G. (1995). *Reading difficulties: Instruction and assessment* (2nd ed.). New York: McGraw-Hill.

Comparison–Contrast Chart and Venn Diagram

EL Beneficial when working with English learners

Strategy at a Glance: *Grade Levels All*			
When to Use	**Grouping**	**Literature Type**	**Skill Areas**
○ before reading	● individual	● narrative	○ word recognition
○ during reading	● small group	● expository	● vocabulary
● after reading	● whole class		● comprehension
	○ center		● writing

Purpose

To understand similarities and differences (or comparison–contrast) of events, ideas, or characters

Literature Used

A River Ran Wild, by Lynne Cherry

Pink and Say, by Patricia Polacco

Next Year I'll Be Special, by Patricia Reilly Giff

When to Use

After reading

Description of Strategy

A comparison–contrast chart develops thinking skills as students discover how events, ideas, or characters are alike or different. The teacher creates a three-column chart. Elements of comparison or contrast for two general topics are listed in the center column. One general topic is written at the top of the left column and the other at the top of the right column. After reading, the students compare or contrast the specific elements of what they have read based on the elements given about the two general topics.

Procedures for Use

1. The teacher selects a book (or two books) that offers students an opportunity to compare and contrast.

Major Topic	Elements of Comparison–Contrast	Major Topic

FIGURE 31–1   Example of Generic Comparison–Contrast Chart

2. *Before* reading, the teacher sets a purpose for reading by teaching the concept of comparison and contrast. This concept might be demonstrated with two students—height, outfit, hair color, and so on. This could be done, for example, with differences and similarities between fourth grade last year and fifth grade this year with such elements as homework, classroom, and lunchtime.

3. The teacher and students discuss the examples related to fourth and fifth grade. The teacher encourages active listening as students respond to questions related to comparison and contrast.

4. The teacher shows the students the prepared chart on an overhead or board. (See Figure 31–1.) After modeling the thinking for the first one or two examples, the teacher may let the students complete the chart in pairs or triads.

5. Once the background building discussion on comparison–contrast is complete, the teacher reads *A River Ran Wild*. The teacher instructs students to listen for differences in the thoughts of Native Americans and the thoughts of settlers, according to the book. (See Figure 31–2.)

6. *After* reading, the teacher distributes the prepared chart. The teacher may model the first item and let students complete the chart in cooperative learning groups. (See Figure 31–3 for another version of a comparison–contrast for Patricia Polacco's *Pink and Say*.)

Indians (Native Americans)	Elements of Comparison–Contrast	Settlers (Non-Native Americans)
	use of animals	
	animal "feelings"	
	flow of the river	
	use of trees	
	land ownership	
	river ownership	
	care of natural resources	

FIGURE 31–2   Example of Comparison–Contrast Chart for *A River Ran Wild*

Pinkus	Elements of Comparison–Contrast	Sheldon
Pink	nickname	Say
	race	
	Union military weapons used	
	fought for the Union	
	education (reading)	
	prisoner of war	

FIGURE 31–3   Example of Comparison–Contrast Chart for *Pink and Say*

Alternate Idea

When first introducing comparison–contrast organization, teachers may want to use a Venn diagram. This graphic organizer has overlapping circles in which each circle represents one of the two items for comparison–contrast. Similar characteristics among the two items go in the overlapping section of the circles. Different characteristics go in the parts of each circle outside the overlapping area.

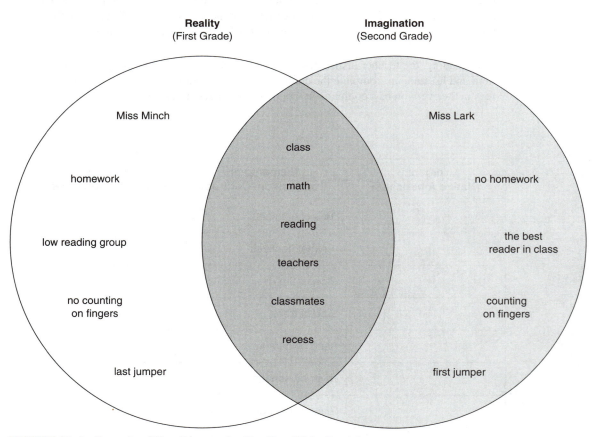

FIGURE 31–4   Example of Venn Diagram for *Next Year I'll Be Special*

After reading a selection like *Pink and Say*, the teacher asks students to *list* ideas that the two main characters share and ideas about each that are different. Students may record these as individuals, within collaborative learning groups, or as a whole-class brainstorming activity. After listing ideas, learners then *group* them into which ones are similar about the two boys and which ones are different. Now students are ready to categorize on the Venn diagram whether an idea is relevant either to Pink or to Say or whether it is something the two have in common. In other words, learners are giving an appropriate *label* to an idea as they record it.

The Venn diagram may serve as a *before* reading activity if the teacher and students were to compare and contrast topics with which learners already possessed the necessary background knowledge, such as two sports. Engaging in such an exercise prepares students with the necessary schema for using the strategy *after* reading for the two characters in a book like *Pink and Say*. Also, the Venn diagram is useful as a prewriting activity to organize ideas before students begin composing drafts for a comparison–contrast paragraph or longer essay.

The example in Figure 31–4 provides an illustration of a Venn diagram for Patricia Reilly Giff's *Next Year I'll Be Special* as a class explored the likenesses and differences between reality and imagination in first and second grades as described in the story. As a graphic organizer, this one helps with vocabulary development, the mental ability of categorization, and understanding the organizational pattern of comparison–contrast.

Further Reading

Cooper, J. D. (2000). *Literacy: Helping children construct meaning* (4th ed.). Boston: Houghton Mifflin.

Cunningham, P., & Allington, R. (1994). *Classrooms that work.* New York: HarperCollins.

Graves, M., Juel, C., & Graves, B. (1998). *Teaching reading in the 21st century.* Needham Heights, MA: Allyn & Bacon.

Gunning, T. (2005). *Creating literacy instruction for all students* (5th ed.). Boston: Allyn & Bacon.

Harris, A. J., & Sipay, E. R. (1990). *How to increase reading ability: A guide to developmental and remedial methods* (9th ed.). New York: Longman.

Johns, J., & Lenski, S. D. (2001). *Improving reading: Strategies and resources* (3rd ed.). Dubuque, IA: Kendall/Hunt.

Norton, D. E., & Norton, S. E. (2003). *Through the eyes of a child: An introduction to children's literature* (6th ed.). Upper Saddle River, NJ: Merrill/Prentice Hall.

Reutzel, D. R., & Cooter, R. (2000). *Teaching children to read: Putting the pieces together* (3rd ed.). Columbus, OH: Merrill.

Tierney, R. J., & Readence, J. E. (2000). *Reading strategies and practices: A compendium* (5th ed.). Boston: Allyn & Bacon.

Tompkins, G. E. (2005). *Language arts: Patterns of practice* (6th ed.). Upper Saddle River, NJ: Merrill/Prentice Hall.

Vacca, R. T., & Vacca, J. A. L. (2005). *Content area reading: Literacy and learning across the curriculum* (8th ed.). Boston: Allyn & Bacon.

Character Map

EL Beneficial when working with English learners

Strategy at a Glance: *Grade Levels 1–8*			
When to Use	**Grouping**	**Literature Type**	**Skill Areas**
○ before reading	● individual	● narrative	○ word recognition
○ during reading	● small group	● expository	● vocabulary
● after reading	● whole class		● comprehension
	○ center		● writing

Purpose

To aid in recognizing and describing characters

Literature Used

Miss Nelson Has a Field Day, by Harry Allard and James Marshall

When to Use

After reading

Description of Strategy

Character maps are graphic organizers that help identify the different characters in a story and the words used by the writer that describe each character. Words may come from the text to describe the characters, or the words may be implied by the story or the pictures. A thesaurus will help students find synonyms for the descriptive words.

Procedures for Use

1. The teacher should select a book with at least three vibrant characters and no more than six to keep confusion minimal. *Miss Nelson Has a Field Day* has several interesting characters.

2. The teacher reads the story aloud, as students follow along, and directs them to listen for interesting things about the people in the story. At set points in the story, the teacher engages the students in guided listening by briefly pausing to comment on main characters or ask pertinent questions about them.

3. *After* reading the story, the students underline or write on another sheet of paper words or phrases that describe the characters. Students may refer to the book as part of purposeful rereading to learn details about each character.

4. Either the teacher or the students (with teacher guidance) draw a character map. (Refer to Figure 32–1.) The center of the map is a rectangle or any other preferred geometric figure that contains the story title. From the center, arrows radiate and connect to other shapes, usually ovals. Each oval has a character's name written in it. Triangles next radiate from each oval and will have words or phrases selected from the book or generated by the students themselves as descriptions of the various characters. These character descriptions may be stated or implied by the words in the text or suggested by its pictures.

5. A thesaurus will help students find synonyms for the descriptive words from the text and may become part of the character map. If the book says the principal was "goofy," a synonym from a thesaurus that might be added to the chart is "foolish." Use of a thesaurus fosters reader competencies in using reference tools.

6. An alternative approach is to have students draw the map on posterboard with different colored markers for character names and descriptors. The teacher might provide different colors of self-adhesive notes so that character names and descriptors can be removed, mixed up, and placed back on the map. *Inspiration* software draws concept maps. Using this program as another alternative integrates technology into the lesson.

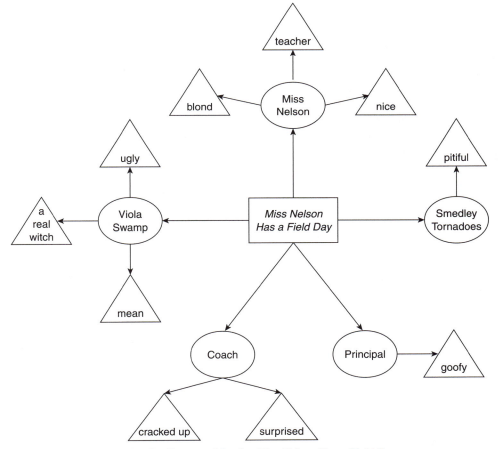

FIGURE 32–1   Example of a Character Map for *Miss Nelson Has a Field Day*

7. The teacher should provide for differences in pupil learning. Less able students may benefit from having a word bank of character names or descriptive words from the story. As an *after* reading extension activity, advanced students can write one or more sentences about a character like Miss Nelson by using the descriptive words found on the character map.

8. This strategy also works well with expository material when a class is studying famous people, places, or things in subject areas besides language arts.

Further Reading

Gipe, J. P. (2006). *Multiple paths to literacy: Assessment and differentiated instruction for diverse learners, K–12* (6th ed.). Upper Saddle River, NJ: Merrill/Prentice Hall.

Gunning, T. G. (2005). *Creating literacy instruction for all students* (5th ed.). Boston: Allyn & Bacon.

Johns, J., & Lenski, S. D. (2001). *Improving reading: Strategies and resources* (3rd ed.). Dubuque, IA: Kendall/Hunt.

Character Sketch

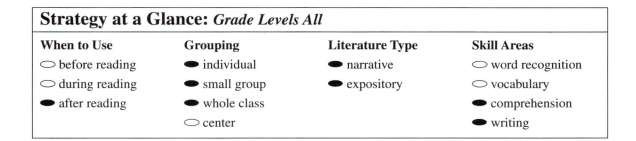
EL Beneficial when working with English learners

Strategy at a Glance: *Grade Levels All*			
When to Use	**Grouping**	**Literature Type**	**Skill Areas**
○ before reading	● individual	● narrative	○ word recognition
○ during reading	● small group	● expository	○ vocabulary
● after reading	● whole class		● comprehension
	○ center		● writing

Purpose

To describe the thoughts, actions, experiences, and feelings of a character in a story

Literature Used

I Am Rosa Parks, by Rosa Parks

When to Use

After reading

Description of Strategy

A character sketch allows students to think about and write about a character's thoughts, feelings, actions, and experiences. The teacher duplicates a silhouette of a whole person or has students draw a silhouette of a person. *After* reading about someone, students will write about the person's thoughts in the head of the silhouette. The character's feelings will be written in the trunk (or body) of the silhouette near the heart. Things a character sees or hears may be added near the eyes and ears. Actions the character takes may be recorded on the hands. Places the character goes are added to the feet area. (See Figure 33–1.) Based on the information recorded on the character sketch, an extension of the strategy is for students to compose a summary paragraph for each attribute of the person. For instance, the paragraph could detail feelings taken from the trunk of the sketch.

115

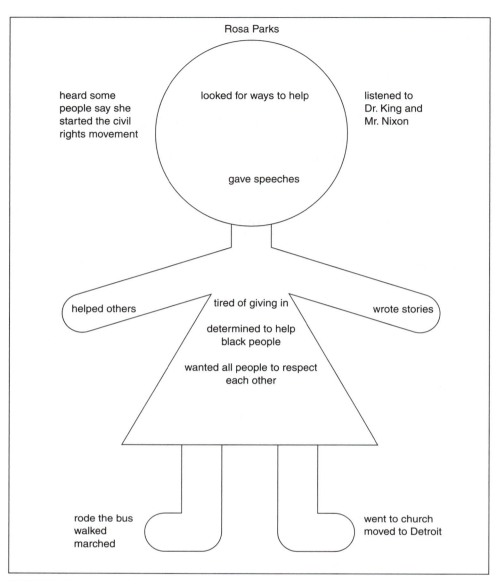

FIGURE 33–1   Example of a Character Sketch for *I Am Rosa Parks*

Procedures for Use

1. *Before* reading the story, the teacher should lead a discussion about how classmates have gotten to know each other. Remarks might include knowing classmates by what they do, what they say, or where they go. The teacher might use one student as an example. The teacher could explain that writers sometimes want readers to know about the people in a story, so readers have to pay attention to what writers say about the characters.

2. As a way to build background for the character sketch strategy, the teacher should show the book, *I Am Rosa Parks,* and may want to state, "This book is an autobiography. That means Rosa Parks wanted you to know her story, so she wrote this book." The teacher sets a purpose by telling students to listen *during* reading to learn as many details about Rosa Parks as they can remember.

3. *After* reading, the teacher shows Rosa Parks' silhouette on a poster and prompts the students to remember some places Ms. Parks went. Class responses are written by the

teacher on the feet of the silhouette. Prompts for the discussion about Rosa Parks might include questions like these: "What are some things she saw? What is something she heard? What did she do to help others?" As the students offer ideas from the text, the teacher models writing other responses on body parts of the silhouette.

4. Upon completing the silhouette with relevant details, students can use it to guide their writing of one or more paragraphs about the character. Like many graphic organizers, the character sketch functions as a prewriting outline for ordering one's thoughts.

5. This strategy works well collaboratively with a partner or small groups as well as independently for character study.

Further Reading

Carmine, D., Silbert, S., Kame'enui, E. J., Tarver, S. G., & Jungjohann, K. (2006). *Teaching struggling and at-risk readers: A direct instruction approach.* Columbus, OH: Merrill/Prentice Hall.

Gipe, J. P. (2006). *Multiple paths to literacy: Assessment and differentiated instruction for diverse learners, K–12* (6th ed.). Upper Saddle River, NJ: Merrill/Prentice Hall.

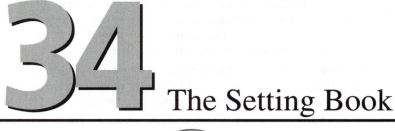

The Setting Book

EL Beneficial when working with English learners

Strategy at a Glance: *Grade Levels 2–6*			
When to Use	**Grouping**	**Literature Type**	**Skill Areas**
● before reading	○ individual	● narrative	○ word recognition
○ during reading	● small group	○ expository	○ vocabulary
● after reading	○ whole class		● comprehension
	○ center		● writing

Purpose

To help students determine the setting(s) of a particular piece of literature.

Literature Used

When I Was Young in the Mountains, by Cynthia Rylant

When to Use

Before and after reading

Description of Strategy

The setting book helps readers remember the setting(s) of a particular book they are reading. After the teacher activates prior knowledge about the where and when of setting, students will listen to the teacher read a book and answer questions about the setting. They will record their answers under each letter of the setting book. It has three pages. The first two pages have seven equal slits left to right. The slits are positioned so that they may be raised to reveal questions underneath. The first page, or the cover, has each letter of the word "setting" on each of the separate seven slits. The second page has questions related to student experiences and is used *before* reading. To illustrate the strategy with a specific story, the third page has questions from *When I Was Young in the Mountains* and is completed *after* reading.

Procedures for Use

1. The teacher prepares a setting book for each student. (See Figure 34–1.) Under each letter of the word "setting," questions will help activate student prior knowledge *before* reading. Questions include "Where do you go to sleep at night?" under the letter **s** "Where do you eat breakfast in the morning?" under the letter **e** "Where do you watch television?" under the letter **t** and so forth. Each student may have different answers. Students record their answers under each letter on the second page of the setting book where the prompts are. The teacher will explain to the students that the answers to each of their questions will be a setting. For example, the setting where the class is would be the classroom or perhaps the room number.

2. After each student has completed the second page of the book, the teacher will call on a few students to share their answers. Once sharing is done, the students will put their setting books aside, and the teacher will read *When I Was Young in the Mountains* by Cynthia Rylant. The teacher tells the students to listen for setting changes.

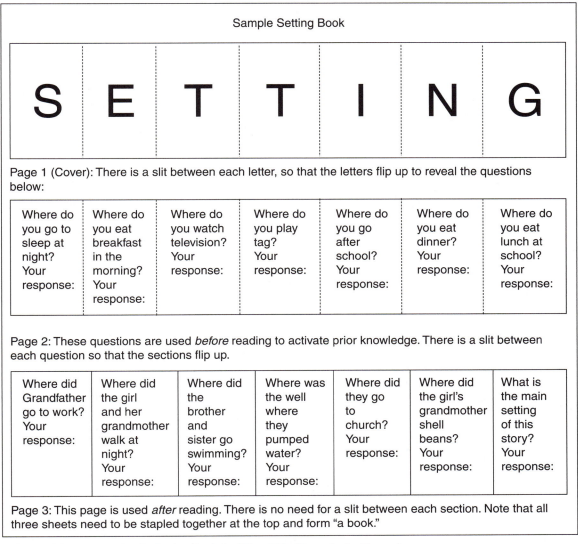

FIGURE 34–1   Example of a Setting Book for *When I Was Young in the Mountains*

3. *After* reading the book to the class, the teacher asks students to get out their setting books. The third page of the book will contain questions about the setting of *When I Was Young in the Mountains*. The teacher will model how to answer the first question for the students. For guided practice, the teacher and students will complete the second question (under the "e") together. The class will do the rest of the book independently. Once students have finished, they may choose a partner and compare answers.

4. If less able learners are in the classroom, the teacher may work with these students or provide a concept bank from which they may select answers.

Further Reading

Frey, N., & Fisher, D. B. (2006). *Language arts workshop: Purposeful reading and writing instruction*. Columbus, OH: Pearson Prentice Hall.

Gipe, J. P. (2006). *Multiple paths to literacy: Assessment and differentiated instruction for diverse learners, K–12* (6th ed.). Upper Saddle River, NJ: Merrill/Prentice Hall.

Gunning, T. (2005). *Creating literacy instruction for all students* (5th ed.). Boston: Allyn & Bacon.

PART V

Writing Strategies

Categorization of language arts often falls into two subdivisions: receptive and expressive. The traditional ones included in the first are listening and reading; while in the second are speaking and writing. Because receiving communication and expressing it often occur today through modes other than verbal—actually such has always been the case at least as far back as the cave painting of the Stone Age—viewing is another form of communication and is both expressive and receptive. Human beings receive and express messages visually. Instead of viewing, sometimes the term "mediacy" denominates a fifth language arts component in an effort to be more clearly inclusive of technology as a way to receive and send information.

All of the language arts are interrelated, and growth in one develops growth in the others. Strategies previously discussed in this book promote not only reading but listening, speaking, and writing. A glance back at the sections on vocabulary and comprehension reveals support for this contention. The graphic organizer in Figure 18–1 of Part III, Vocabulary clearly will aid students in organizing a written description of major systems of the body in a life science class, and the plot-relationship chart in Figure 24–1 of Part IV, Comprehension is a natural precursor to writing a summary of a narrative selection once students have outlined basic components of its story grammar. If members of a class work together in collaborative learning teams, their discussions in creating these types of graphic representations should help them become better listeners and speakers.

This section focuses on selected strategies to foster expressive facility in writing, particularly guided writing where learners generate ideas based on reading a text whether in language arts classes or in content areas, then organize these ideas, and finally revise and edit them into a written product. The emphasis is thus on process and product. References to the steps of "list, group, label" form part of the process of generating and organizing thoughts as a component of class discussions. The description given in Strategy 12 of this book on Concept of Definition discusses these steps more fully. Also of note is that the writing strategies concentrate on expressing content over strict grammatical correctness, the latter usually more part of revision, although both communication of content and grammar are important.

As part of instruction, teachers should help students realize why writing is useful to them. Communicating for authentic, functional purposes is a way to instill such understanding. Sending a text message or thank you note, creating an academic report, completing a flyer for neighborhood babysitting or possible yard work, requesting that the school administration allow more time for locker access, or developing a school guide for new students are valuable reasons for writing for authentic purposes.

As Part I, Creating Successful Literacy Lessons makes clear and as is emphasized in the strategies here, teacher modeling through direct instruction is important. In addition, once students have engaged in initial efforts in the writing process, teachers should have conferences that offer encouragement and thought-provoking suggestions, alternatives, or questions for learners to ponder in order to solve communication problems. These conferences should occur before students complete their written products. Peer review of written work may be beneficial when the focus is on providing helpful coaching comments or positive corrective feedback rather than negative criticism.

For developing writers, these strategies provide much in the way of structure to give needed scaffolding and sheltered instruction to aid in creating successful writing experiences. All teachers want students who can read and write effortlessly, but most, if not all, students need years of guidance and encouragement, a circumstance that is both the teacher's challenge and satisfaction.

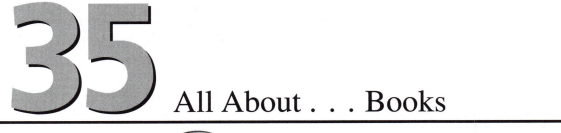

35 All About . . . Books

EL Beneficial when working with English learners

Strategy at a Glance: *Grade Levels All*			
When to Use	**Grouping**	**Literature Type**	**Skill Areas**
● before reading	● individual	● narrative	○ word recognition
● during reading	● small group	● expository	● vocabulary
● after reading	● whole class		● comprehension
	○ center		● writing

Purpose

To integrate reading, writing, and visual literacy through narrative text or through expository text

Literature Used

Prudence's Book of Food, by Alona Frankel
My Many Colored Days, by Dr. Seuss

When to Use

Before, during, and after reading

Description of Strategy

All About . . . Books may impart information as students write narratives about themselves or as they discuss informational topics in an expository mode of expression. In the first instance of narratives, All About . . . Books, done as autobiographies, are referred to as All About Me Books and give personal information such as date of birth; descriptions of family members, friends, pets, and other significant associates; favorite activities and books; interests; and so forth. In the second instance, if written as expository text about nonpersonal topics, All About . . . Books may be on such subjects studied in content areas as presidents, weather phenomena, insects, the circulatory system, a particular city like San Francisco, and so forth. In either case, illustrations accompany both types of All About . . . Books and allow students to express ideas through visual communication as well as through writing. These books also may aid students in developing strategic study competencies as they organize their final products into appropriate sections that include a title page, table of contents, numbered pages with synchronized words and pictures, and perhaps a bibliography of informational sources used in creating their work.

Procedures for Use

1. The teacher should select literature that will serve as a model for composing an All About . . . Book. For preschool and early primary age children, Alona Frankel's *Prudence's Book of Food* is appropriate for the content area of health and would serve as an example for learners to explore appropriate and inappropriate foods to eat. For older primary and intermediate-grade students, Dr. Seuss's *My Many Colored Days* would be a good choice for an autobiographical All About Me Book that discusses different personal feelings they have from time to time as these relate to moods of color.

2. *Before* reading, the teacher shares either story (or another one) with the students. As students listen, the teacher reads *aloud* and pauses to discuss how the pictures complement and supplement the meaning of the words. Students should feel free to join the discussion and add their own interpretations of pictures and words. For instance, with *My Many Colored Days,* students might describe how they react to what Dr. Seuss calls "Bright Red Days" or "Happy Pink" days.

3. The teacher may want to revisit the selected text a second time *during* reading by having the listeners join in as they read *along*. For extra practice, a third reading could occur as students read *alone* without the teacher's assistance. This shared mode of reading provides multiple exposures to the book's words.

4. Proceeding from literary models, the teacher and students now create either an All About . . . Books or an All About Me Book. If *Prudence's Book of Food* has been the model, preschool and early primary grade children may describe other types of appropriate edible foods for the content area of health. Their books might be titled *All About Foods.* If *My Many Colored Days* is the choice, primary or intermediate-grade students could title their works *All About My Many Colored Feelings.* Both works would have at least a single sentence or caption per page, and each page would have an accompanying illustration.

5. For whichever type of book students compose, the teacher may want to scaffold the writing through the language experience approach (LEA) as part of *after* reading. Working with individuals, small groups, or a whole class, the teacher engages learners in a conversation about the book's content (i.e., what kinds of foods to include and discuss or what types of personal feelings to match with different colors. (See pages 23–25 to find out more about the language experience approach.) Once learners reach consensus about content, they dictate to the teacher their captions for each page. The teacher records these on the chalkboard, chart paper, or overhead projector and reads the words *aloud* as students see their ideas unfold and thus develop competence in word recognition. Next, the teacher and students read *along* together the recorded text. Finally, students will read the captions *alone*. More advanced students may be able to write the captions themselves and create their books independently.

6. The teacher may direct students to a computer to use a word processing program to reproduce the captions in typed print. The teacher will begin by showing the student the different fonts on the computer. This procedure will help students to realize that words can look different if typed in different types of print. Then, students will read each caption while the teacher types it. Finally, the teacher and students will print out the captions. Students will cut out each caption and glue it to match the appropriate picture they have

created for their books. Instead of drawings, some students may want to illustrate their captions with photographs.

7. The teacher should make sure that the books, whether by individuals, small groups, or the whole class, are bound in some form. Pages might be connected with a plastic spiral ring binding. Books may be bound individually, or all may be bound as a class project for sharing with others whether students, parents, teachers, or administrators.

Further Reading

Tompkins, G. E. (2005). *Language arts: Patterns of practice* (6th ed.). Upper Saddle River, NJ: Merrill/Prentice Hall.

36 Story Impressions

EL Beneficial when working with English learners

Strategy at a Glance: *Grade Levels All*			
When to Use	**Grouping**	**Literature Type**	**Skill Areas**
● before reading	● individual	● narrative	○ word recognition
○ during reading	● small group	○ expository	● vocabulary
● after reading	○ whole class		● comprehension
	○ center		● writing

Purpose

To use clues to predict and then write story events that students later compare to the original story

Literature Used

Piggie Pie, by Margerie Palanti

When to Use

Before and after reading

Description of Strategy

Story impressions stir the curiosity of learners and activate their prior knowledge as they use teacher-provided clues to predict and construct their versions of a story *before* reading the original. Story impressions include key words or phrases of one, two, or three words related to the original story. These key words should represent character, setting, and major elements from the plot. The teacher should restrict the number of key words or phrases to approximately 10 to 15 for a short story or picture book and to around 15 to 20 for a chapter book. The clues should be arranged vertically with arrows or lines to indicate the sequence. The teacher should stress that students use the words in the order that they appear. Otherwise, students may get the events out of sequence. Story impressions become guideposts from which students make predictions or ask questions *before* reading.

Students use their background knowledge to hypothesize the story events. Working in small groups of three or four, they create their own story by recording the events. They then compare their rendition to the original story *after* reading it. Through arousing curiosity and building background, the strategy of story impressions enhances literacy competencies of prediction, understanding sequence, writing, and comparison–contrast.

Procedures for Use

1. The teacher shows the book *Piggie Pie* to the students.
2. Next, the teacher provides a general introduction such as, "Today we will make up what we think this story is about."
3. The teacher focuses student attention on the list of key concepts by saying, "Here are some clues about the story, *Piggie Pie,* that we will read." (See Figure 36–1.) "We will use these

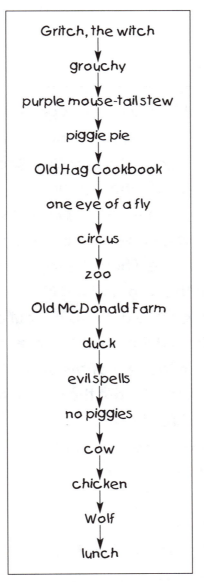

Gritch, the witch

↓

grouchy

↓

purple mouse-tail stew

↓

piggie pie

↓

Old Hag Cookbook

↓

one eye of a fly

↓

circus

↓

zoo

↓

Old McDonald Farm

↓

duck

↓

evil spells

↓

no piggies

↓

cow

↓

chicken

↓

Wolf

↓

lunch

FIGURE 36–1   Example of Clues for *Piggie Pie*

clues to write our own version of the story. After that, we will read the story together to see if the author had similar ideas to ours."

4. After the students read the list of clues, they brainstorm, in small collaborative groups, about how the ideas might connect. The teacher lists the possibilities on the overhead or board.

5. The teacher allows the students to work in groups to come up with their own stories. (The students may work on a story individually.)

6. Using the brainstormed ideas, students develop a story that ties together the clues. (See Figure 36–2.)

7. The students read the author's actual story and discuss how their story compares and contrasts. A match with the author is **not** important. Instead, it is important to understand how the clues are woven together similarly or differently.

8. As an extension or follow-up activity for independent practice, students could work either in small groups or as individuals to develop stories based on clues from another text.

> Gritch the witch was grouchy. She put purple mouse tails in her stew. She put a pig in her pie. She made a gross witches cookbook. She was grouchy because she had to take the pie and stew to a lot of places. She took an eye out of a fly for the recipe. Then she took it to the circus, then the Zoo and Old McDonald Farm. She fed it to a duck. She put evil spells in it. She did not feed it to pigs. She put a cow in the rest of the stew. She fed it to a chicken. She put the wolf in the piggie pie. While she was eating lunch, she put an extra spell just for her and it made her un-grouchy.
>
> By: Shelbi   Grade 3

FIGURE 36–2   Example of Student Version for *Piggie Pie*

Further Reading

Gipe, J. P. (2006). *Multiple paths to literacy: Assessment and differentiated instruction for diverse learners, K–12* (6th ed.). Upper Saddle River, NJ: Merrill/Prentice Hall.

Johns, J., & Lenski, S. D. (2001). *Improving reading: Strategies and resources* (3rd ed.). Dubuque, IA: Kendall/Hunt.

Tierney, R. J., & Readence, J. E. (2000). *Reading strategies and practices: A compendium* (5th ed.). Boston: Allyn & Bacon.

Vacca, J. A. L., Vacca, R. T., & Gove, M. K. (2000). *Reading and learning to read* (4th ed.). New York: Addison Wesley Longman.

Vacca, R. T., & Vacca, J. A. L. (2005). *Content area reading: Literacy and learning across the curriculum* (8th ed.). Boston: Allyn & Bacon.

37

Rewriting a Story from Another Point of View

EL Beneficial when working with English learners

Strategy at a Glance: *Grade Levels 4–8*

When to Use	Grouping	Literature Type	Skill Areas
○ before reading	● individual	● narrative	○ word recognition
○ during reading	● small group	● expository	○ vocabulary
● after reading	○ whole class		● comprehension
	○ center		● writing

Purpose

To promote understanding of the literary elements of genre, point of view, style, and character through writing

Literature Used

"The Frogs Who Wanted a King," by Aesop

When to Use

After reading

Description of Strategy

Genre, point of view, style, and character are important literary components for students to comprehend as they develop literary appreciation. All of these may be enhanced through writing activities in which students create their own versions of another story. As learners study genres such as fables, legends, myths, folktales, historical fiction, biography, modern realism, and others, they learn characteristics peculiar to each type of literature. In studying fables, students learn that these stories are usually short narratives, often having animal but sometimes human characters, and that the stories teach a life truth in the form of a moral either stated or implied.

Students also learn in their literature program about point of view, the four common types being omniscient, limited omniscient, first person, and objective. In the omniscient point of view, the narrator is all-knowing, capable of recounting not only all of the characters' actions and conversations but also their thoughts and feelings. The narrator tells about the story characters and speaks in third person. In the limited omniscient viewpoint, the narrator also speaks in third person, but this time reveals the thoughts and feelings of only one character. For all other characters, the narrator is limited to reporting action and dialogue. First person point of view elevates one of the characters in the story to the status of narrator and uses first person pronouns like "I," "we," "our," and "us." The narrator is an eyewitness to the story's events or reports events from hearsay passed on by other characters. In the objective point of view, the narrator returns to third person but reports just the facts and omits any personal interpretation so that readers must draw their own conclusions as to the meaning of events. Sometimes called the dramatic point of view, this form of telling a story is limited to conversation and action as in watching a play from which listeners must infer what characters think and feel.

Style of writing—that is, diction, sentence structure, imagery, and atmosphere—are all governed by point of view. Thus, a story told in first person may have a highly different style from one told in omniscient or objective point of view. If students rewrite in first person a genre story like the Aesop fable "The Frogs Who Wanted a King," they have the opportunity to experiment with word choice, sentence structure, figures of speech, and atmosphere as they transform a story originally told in omniscient point of view.

Procedures for Use

1. The teacher makes certain that students are thoroughly familiar with the original story—in this case, "The Frogs Who Wanted a King."
2. Other familiar children's stories and interpretations may also be discussed and shared with learners. These provide authentic models of how to write a different version of the same story.
3. An example to use for modeling rewriting may be "The Story of the Three Little Pigs" and some of the recent retellings. These examples are shared with students. The teacher may read aloud or have children read variations like Eugene Trivizas' *The Three Little Wolves and the Big Bad Pig,* illustrated by Helen Oxenbury; or Jon Scieszka's *The True Story of the Three Little Pigs! By A. Wolf,* illustrated by Lane Smith. The first version provides a model for rewriting the original story, while the second version demonstrates how one of the characters (the wolf) from the original tells his side of the story.
4. Once sufficient modeling and background building have occurred, students will be ready to rewrite the story under consideration. Figure 37–1 shows the original version of "The Frogs Who Wanted a King." It is followed by an example of an eighth grader's rendition in first person, with Zeus telling his side of things. The student's rewritten version in first person narrative uses a haughty style appropriate to the all-powerful Zeus and thereby conveys the disdain of the god for the bothersome frogs.

Aesop's "The Frogs Who Wanted a King"

Some frogs who lived in a pond were bored with freedom, so they sent a petition to Zeus and asked to be given a king. Although the god thought the frogs better off as they were, to oblige them he hurled a log into their pond. Hearing the splash, the frogs were terrified, and scurried to the pond's far corners. But by and by, seeing that the log lay motionless, they approached, and growing bolder said to one another, "What, is this our powerful king?" Soon they were jumping out of the water and squatting on the log, croaking in contempt.

After a while, they tired of this sport. Again, some of them went to Zeus and asked him to get rid of such a lazy, do-nothing king and send them a more forceful one. Annoyed, Zeus caused a great stork to descend to the pond. Frogs were his favorite food.

Example of a First Person Retelling of "The Frogs Who Wanted a King"

Dear gods and goddesses,

Let me tell you what these crazy frogs on Earth had the nerve to ask me, Zeus, the greatest god of all. They wanted a king. A king!!! Can you believe that? What could those lowly creatures want with a king? They are too low on the chain of existence to have their own king. Don't they know that I am Zeus, the all-powerful? I can create and destroy at the wiggling of my nose. But I decided to oblige those slimy creatures with their request. So, I thought about it and thought about it. Who or what would be a suitable ruler for those primitive creatures? I had it! I decided to send them a huge log to rule over them. Great idea, huh? This ruler would be understanding and lenient. The frogs could do whatever they wanted. I just knew that they would praise me for the selection I made. You know what I got from these pond dwellers? Nothing but grief. That's right! They said they wanted a forceful king. So, I decided to send a stork, one of the many enemies of all pond suckers. The stork loved his new kingdom, but the frogs didn't like their new king. That's what you get when you bother me when I could be doing better things. That'll learn 'em!

Yours truly,

The All-Powerful Zeus

The All-Powerful Zeus

FIGURE 37–1   Original Version and First Person Retelling of "The Frogs Who Wanted a King"

Further Reading

Donelson, K. L., & Nilsen, A. P. (1997). *Literature for today's young adults* (5th ed.). New York: Addison Wesley Longman.

Norton, D. E., & Norton, S. E. (2003). *Through the eyes of a child: An introduction to children's literature* (6th ed.). Upper Saddle River, NJ: Merrill/Prentice Hall.

Tompkins, G. E. (2005). *Language arts: Patterns of Practice* (6th ed.). Upper Saddle River, NJ: Merrill/Prentice Hall.

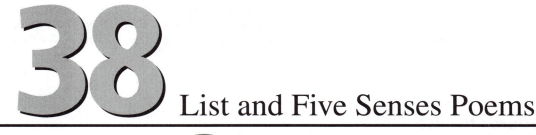

List and Five Senses Poems

EL Beneficial when working with English learners

Strategy at a Glance: *Grade Levels All*			
When to Use	**Grouping**	**Literature Type**	**Skill Areas**
○ before reading	● individual	● narrative	○ word recognition
○ during reading	● small group	● expository	● vocabulary
● after reading	○ whole class		● comprehension
	○ center		● writing

Purpose

To develop literary appreciation for poetry, to teach main idea and detail organization in writing, and to enhance comprehension of narrative or expository text

Literature Used

"Swift things are beautiful . . . ," by Elizabeth Coatsworth, in *The Scott, Foresman Anthology of Children's Literature,* eds. Zena Sutherland and Myra Cohn Livingston

"Thanksgiving," by Ivy O. Eastwick, in *Ring Out Wild Bells: Poems about Holidays and Seasons,* ed. Lee Bennett Hopkins

When to Use

After reading

Description of Strategy

List poems help students to understand main idea-detail relationships and are one of the easiest kinds of poems to compose if learners are reluctant writers of poetry. Scaffolding of the writing process occurs through the formula that list poems follow. The key component of the formula is a verse paragraph structured according to a main idea and supporting details. The opening line(s) should convey a main idea statement usually in the form of a central image for each stanza of the poem. Students then list images that support the main idea of the key image.

Five senses poems follow the same structural concept as list poems, except that more scaffolding is provided through organizing each line around one of the five senses. These guide students in composing their list of images or figures of speech (namely, the details) for their verse paragraph.

Procedures for Use

1. For a list poem minus the five senses, Elizabeth Coatsworth's two stanzas of "Swift things are beautiful . . ." provide learners with a strong literary model. The opening line of the first verse illustrates its main idea: "Swift things are beautiful. . . ." The teacher makes this point with students.

2. The teacher then demonstrates how the remaining lines of the stanza contain a list of supporting details: swallows, deer, lightning, rivers, meteors, wind, horses, and runners. Although the poem rhymes, this feature is not necessary for students to include.

3. The next stanza of the poem begins with a contrasting main idea: "And slow things are beautiful. . . ." Again, a list of images follows containing details to support this main idea. Among these are the end of the day, the slow dying embers of a fire, the blooming of flowers, and a slow-moving ox.

4. After students have studied the structure of the main idea and supporting details, they may write their own list poems about topics studied in narrative or expository text. For example, they might compose a list poem about a main character in a story, a historical figure, a geographical place, or a concept in science or math.

5. For students who need additional scaffolding in writing a list poem, the teacher can show them how to incorporate images related to each of the five senses. Ivy O. Eastwick's "Thanksgiving" provides a good model if this way of structuring a list poem is used.

6. The teacher calls students' attention to the main idea of "Thanksgiving": namely, that each of the three stanzas has the key concept of being thankful for many of life's gifts. Although not all of the five senses are present, the first verse paragraph has the central idea of what the speaker in the poem is thankful for that "my hands can hold"; the second stanza for what "my eyes can see"; and the third for what "my ears can hear." Appropriate images follow as details to convey thankfulness for touch, sight, and sound in each stanza, respectively.

7. Once the teacher demonstrates the list structure related to the senses, students can create their own list poems around one or all of the five senses. The example from a second grader shown in Figure 38–1 is a five senses list poem about the main idea that "War is black." The teacher provided scaffolding by giving the students a simile for each sense listed for their chosen main ideas. These are "looks like," "tastes like," "feels like," "sounds like," and "smells like."

War

War is black.
War looks like bullets going through your heart.
War tastes like sand in your mouth.
War feels like a punch in the face.
War sounds like cannonballs whistling.
War smells like gas bombs.

FIGURE 38–1   Example of a Five Senses List Poem

Further Reading

Cunningham, P., & Allington, R. (1994). *Classrooms that work.* New York: HarperCollins.

Norton, D. E., & Norton, S. E. (2003). *Through the eyes of a child: An introduction to children's literature* (6th ed.). Upper Saddle River, NJ: Merrill/Prentice Hall.

Tompkins, G. E. (2005). *Language arts: Patterns of practice* (6th ed.). Upper Saddle River, NJ: Merrill/Prentice Hall.

39 Scamper

EL Beneficial when working with English learners

Strategy at a Glance: *Grade Levels All*

When to Use	Grouping	Literature Type	Skill Areas
○ before reading	● individual	● narrative	○ word recognition
○ during reading	● small group	● expository	● vocabulary
● after reading	○ whole class		● comprehension
	○ center		● writing

Purpose

To provide students with prompts to enhance creative rewriting opportunities about literature they have read

Literature Used

Cinderella (traditional)

The Egyptian Cinderella, by Shirley Climo

Cinder Edna, by Ellen Jackson

The Rough-Face Girl, by Rafe Martin

When to Use

After reading

Description of Strategy

SCAMPER is an acronym to help writers think of possible stories that could happen if the original version were modified in some way. Each letter in SCAMPER represents a word that helps learners with ideas for creative rewriting. The letters in SCAMPER represent the following: **S** for substitute, **C** for combine, **A** for adapt, **M** for modify, **P** for put to use, **E** for eliminate, and **R** for rearrange or reverse.

Procedures for Use

1. The teacher discusses with students the traditional story of Cinderella and encourages them to point out how other versions read are similar to and different from the traditional story.

2. Explaining that writers often create a new story based on another story, the teacher describes how the word SCAMPER can help students to do the same thing.

3. The teacher goes through each letter of SCAMPER, explaining what each letter stands for and giving an example for each letter.

4. If SCAMPER is used with Cinderella stories, the following prompts are possibilities. Usually, the student selects only one or two of these to aid with rewriting:

   S substitute

   (What if Cinderella lost her handkerchief instead of her shoe?)

   C combine

   (What do Cinderella and Cinder Edna have in common? Can the two stories be combined in some way?)

   A adapt

   (What if the music at the ball had been so loud that Cinderella couldn't hear the clock strike midnight?)

   M modify

   (What would happen if the prince never found anyone whose foot fit the slipper?)

   P put to use

   (What will Cinderella do now with her remaining glass slipper?)

   E eliminate

   (What if there were no pumpkins for the godmother to use?)

   R rearrange or reverse

   (What if the godmother showed up after the ball? Begin your story with the marriage of Cinderella and the prince.)

Note: No reference has been found for this strategy; however, the authors have discovered it to be effective.

40 Imagery

Strategy at a Glance: *Grade Levels All*

When to Use	Grouping	Literature Type	Skill Areas
● before reading	● individual	● narrative	○ word recognition
● during reading	● small group	● expository	● vocabulary
● after reading	● whole class		● comprehension
	○ center		● writing

Purpose

To enhance comprehension through writing or visual representation by guiding students in the development of mental images of text content

Literature Used

Owl Moon, by Jane Yolan

When to Use

Before, during, and after reading

Description of Strategy

Sometimes called "imaging" or "visualizing," imagery improves comprehension of text by encouraging students to create mental pictures *before, during,* and *after* reading and can also be a good activity to use *before, during,* and *after* listening to something read aloud by the teacher or other students. Imagery works especially well with descriptive passages in which the writer appeals to the reader's senses of seeing, hearing, feeling, tasting, or smelling. Activating prior knowledge, improving the ability to make predictions and draw inferences, and promoting overall listening and reading comprehension are among the benefits of using imagery. As with any strategy, the teacher should explain to students the purpose of visualization and why it will be beneficial.

Procedures for Use

1. The teacher selects a text rich in descriptive detail and, depending on the maturity and ability of students, reads aloud a sentence, paragraph, or longer passage. The beginning of Jane Yolan's *Owl Moon* is ideal for this purpose. The story describes a cold winter night when a little girl and her pa go owling and the moon makes the night sky shine brightly.

2. The teacher models the visualization process by creating visual images with students. This process occurs through think-aloud discussions. Mental images are then transferred to paper through drawing pictures (visual representation) or through writing. Sometimes, both pictures and writing may be used.

3. After modeling the process, the teacher initiates guided practice by reading another passage from the text and engaging students in a discussion of images that both they and the teacher visualize. Sufficient time should be allowed so that students can form appropriate and accurate images.

4. It is important not to alter the images created by students. However, the teacher may suggest that they reread or listen to the passage again and decide whether it should be expanded and elaborated. These changes can be suggested through the judicious use of cues, prompts, and questions as part of scaffolding.

5. Independent practice should follow once the teacher feels confident that students have received enough scaffolding through guided practice. Again, students should have sufficient time to form images or to revise them through expansion or elaboration. The images may be shared through oral presentation, drawing, or writing, or through all three modes of communication. Figure 40–1 shows a drawing created by a student for the passage at the beginning of *Owl Moon*.

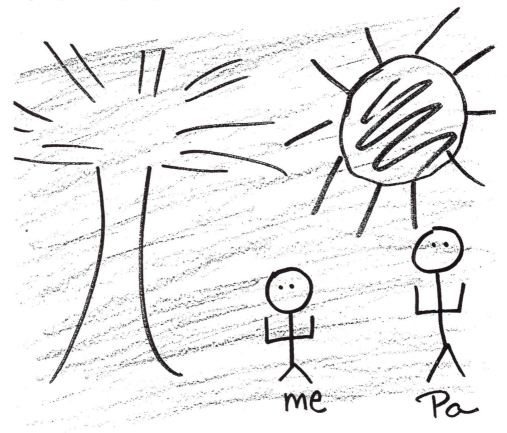

FIGURE 40–1   Example of a Student Visual Representation for the Beginning of *Owl Moon*

Further Reading

Taylor, B., Harris, L. A., Pearson, P. D., & Garcia, G. (1995). *Reading difficulties: Instruction and assessment* (2nd ed.). New York: McGraw-Hill.

Tompkins, G. E. (2005). *Language arts: Patterns of practice* (6th ed.). Upper Saddle River, NJ: Merrill/Prentice Hall.

Vacca, R. T., & Vacca, J. A. L. (2005). *Content area reading: Literacy and learning across the curriculum* (8th ed.). Boston: Allyn & Bacon.

Reluctant Writer

EL Beneficial when working with English learners

Strategy at a Glance: *Grade Levels 1–6*			
When to Use	**Grouping**	**Literature Type**	**Skill Areas**
○ before reading	● individual	● narrative	○ word recognition
○ during reading	○ small group	● expository	○ vocabulary
● after reading	○ whole class		● comprehension
	○ center		● writing

Purpose

To provide scaffolding for children who are reluctant to be writers

Literature Used

Visiting Langston, by Willie Perdomo

When to Use

After reading

Description of Strategy

Some students are hesitant to write, or they lack ideas for writing. This strategy provides scaffolding with specific prompts to help generate ideas for writing.

Procedures for Use

1. The teacher selects either a narrative or expository book or a magazine or newspaper article. The strategy may work best with material that can be interpreted from a variety of viewpoints.

Examples from *Visiting Langston*

Langston Hughes was a writer. (fact)
Mr. Hughes wrote sad poems. (description)
I think he wanted people to be kind to each other. (feeling)

The little girl was a writer. (fact)
She wrote about things she enjoyed like hopscotch and jump rope.
    (description)
She was funny when she said she didn't like catch-n-kiss. (feeling)

FIGURE 41–1   Examples from *Visiting Langston*

2. The teacher introduces the book, *Visiting Langston,* by showing the cover and title pages and by reading the information about Langston Hughes at the beginning of the book.

3. *Before* reading the book aloud, the teacher sets a purpose for listening: "Listen carefully as I read this story aloud. Try to remember facts about Langston Hughes that you can describe and tell how they made you feel."

4. As the students listen, the teacher should stop periodically to encourage them to respond to the text and collage illustrations.

5. *After* reading, the teacher asks the students to look at a transparency showing a written response to the text:

   a. The teacher recalls a *fact* from the book and writes a sentence on a transparency, stating a fact about Langston Hughes. (The teacher may choose to write on a flipchart or the chalkboard.)

   b. The teacher uses a second sentence that *describes* the *fact.*

   c. The teacher writes a third sentence that records a personal *feeling* about the *fact.*

6. Once modeling is completed by the teacher, students may then work with a partner and create a three-sentence paragraph that *states another fact from the book, describes the fact, and gives a feeling about the fact.* Figure 41–1 shows modeling of a fact, description, and feeling written by the teacher. These are followed by a fact, description, and feeling written by a student team.

Further Reading

Cunningham, P., & Allington, R. (1994). *Classrooms that work.* New York: HarperCollins.

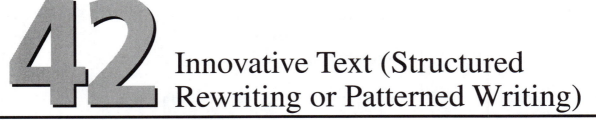

Innovative Text (Structured Rewriting or Patterned Writing)

EL Beneficial when working with English learners

Strategy at a Glance: *Grade Levels All*

When to Use	Grouping	Literature Type	Skill Areas
○ before reading	● individual	● narrative	○ word recognition
○ during reading	● small group	● expository	○ vocabulary
● after reading	○ whole class		● comprehension
	○ center		● writing

Purpose

To provide students a partially completed framework or patterns for rewriting a familiar text to create individual innovations on it

Literature Used

"There Was an Old Lady" in *The Real Mother Goose Book of American Rhymes,* ed. Debby Slier

"Twinkle Twinkle Little Star" in *Jane Yolan's Mother Goose Songbook,* ed. Jane Yolan

When to Use

After reading

Description of Strategy

The teacher selects a song or poem with which students are likely familiar. After the original text is read or sung, the teacher deletes key words. Students then work in small groups to create a new version by filling in alternative words in the blanks.

Procedures for Use

1. The teacher selects a familiar song ("Twinkle, Twinkle Little Star") and additional literature, such as "There Was an Old Lady," that can be adapted to fit this strategy.

2. Once the students are reminded of the song or poem, the teacher explains that the class will be rewriting it. For example, the teacher could show the words to "Twinkle, Twinkle Little Star" on a transparency, chart, or board. Students sing the song as the teacher points

There was an _____ _____ , she swallowed a _____ .

I don't know why she swallowed a _____ .

Perhaps she'll _____ .

There was an _____ _____ , she swallowed a _____ .

It _____ and_____ and _____ inside her.

She swallowed the _____ to catch the _____ .

I don't know why she swallowed a _____ .

Perhaps she'll _____ .

FIGURE 42–1   Example for "There Was an Old Lady"

to the words. The teacher then displays the same song with key words deleted as illustrated below:

_____, _____ little _____,

How I wonder _____ _____ _____.

_____ _____ the world so _____

Like a _____ _____ _____ _____.

_____, _____ little _____,

How I wonder _____ _____ _____.

Oral responses from the students are recorded after they have discussed some possibilities for filling in the blanks.

Gliding, gliding little boat,

How I wonder how you float.

Moving in the world so wide

Like a fish who tries to hide.

Gliding, gliding little boat,

How I wonder how you float.

3. After this scaffolding has occurred, the teacher reads aloud the poem "There Was an Old Lady."

4. After listening, the class will have a copy of the words to the poem with key words deleted. Students work together to fill in the blanks. After writing, the groups may share the new version. (See Figure 42–1.)

5. Students can continue filling in blanks from other verses of this poem, since it continues for many stanzas, if the teacher wants them to.

Further Reading

Cooper, J. D. (2000). *Literacy: Helping children construct meaning* (4th ed.). Boston: Houghton Mifflin.

Cunningham, P. (2000). *Phonics they use* (3rd ed.). New York: Longman.

Cunningham, P., & Allington, R. (1994). *Classrooms that work.* New York: HarperCollins.

Reutzel, D. R., & Cooter, R. (2000). *Teaching children to read: Putting the pieces together* (3rd ed.). Columbus, OH: Merrill.

43

Concept Guides with Graphic Organizers for Main Idea-Detail Relationships

EL Beneficial when working with English learners

Strategy at a Glance: *Grade Levels All*

When to Use	Grouping	Literature Type	Skill Areas
● before reading	● individual	○ narrative	○ word recognition
● during reading	● small group	● expository	○ vocabulary
● after reading	● whole class		● comprehension
	○ center		● writing

Purpose

To focus attention on the hierarchical arrangement of ideas (main ideas and supporting details) in written text

Literature Used

Scott Foresman Science, by Timothy Cooney and others

When to Use

Before, during, and after reading

Description of Strategy

Concept guides develop the notion that information is organized into superordinate concepts (main ideas) that have supportive subordinate details. These guides help students distinguish that some concepts are more important than others and that subordinate details may be categorized under dominate concepts that are main ideas. Concept guides consist of two parts. The first part asks students to recall important supportive details from a passage. The second part requires that these details be categorized under logical main idea headings. This portion of the guide seems to work best for less able learners when it is constructed in the form of a graphic organizer like the ones in this book for a thinking tree, semantic map or web, or closed sort where the teacher has partially completed the graphic organizer to provide extra scaffolding. (See Figures 13–1, 14–1, and 17–1, respectively.)

Procedures for Use

1. The teacher analyzes a passage of text for hierarchical order where subordinate details are categorized within major concepts. The passage should contain key ideas that students need to learn and that they would more readily learn by determining the main idea-detail relationships within the text.

2. The teacher defines what is meant by the main idea and details. The main idea of a passage is the overall concept around which the passage is organized. The details of the passage should be related to the main idea and provide examples, elaboration, or support for it. The teacher next models through a think-aloud how to select the main idea and supporting details for a sample passage before students work through a concept guide so that they will have had schema built for using the strategy.

3. For the first part of the concept guide, the teacher selects key supportive details that logically may be grouped later into main idea headings. The important details are written in the form of statements to which students react by putting a ✓ beside the statement if contained in the reading. Students put an **X** beside statements not in the reading. (See Figure 43–1, Part A, for examples of key details derived from the sections, "How Do Insects and Spiders Grow?" and "How Do Fishes, Frogs, and Mammals Grow?" from the third-grade text, *Scott Foresman Science.*)

4. Upon completing the first part of the concept guide on important details, the teacher develops the second part that requires categorization of information into superordinate, coordinate, and subordinate levels of support. Figure 43–1, Part B, contains the superordinate concept "life cycles." "Mammal," "amphibian," and "insect" are subordinate to it but are coordinate with one another. "Frog" is provided as an additional subordinate detail to its superordinate category "amphibian" so as to give further scaffolding.

5. To complete Part B, students select details from the concept bank (Figure 43–1) and place them under logical main idea categories. As added scaffolding, the word bank lets students know that some details may be used more than once as is indicated by the number in parentheses following "butterfly," "adult," and "egg."

6. While the concept guide in Figure 43–1 was used as an *after* reading review activity, a good idea in using concept guides with students is to have them preview the guide *before* they begin the assigned reading so they will read for a purpose. *During* reading, they complete the guide to help them navigate and organize main idea-detail relationships. *After* reading, students may verify the accuracy with which they completed the guide through discussion in small collaborative learning groups or through whole group verification under the guidance of the teacher. Such multiple exposures to the important information from the text will help implant it into long-term memory more efficiently than would merely assigning pages to read minus the scaffolding of the concept guide.

7. Once students have finished the graphic organizer part of the guide, the teacher may want to have them construct paragraphs with main ideas and supportive details. This writing extension based on what students have read will reinforce the learning of content information and teach the important study strategy of summarizing.

8. Some teachers and students may prefer to use a helping hand visual as an alternative to the graphic organizer in Part B of Figure 43–1. Figure 43–2 shows how a helping

Concept Guide for "How Do Spiders and Insects Grow" and "How Do Fishes, Frogs, and Mammals Grow?"

Part A

Directions: Look at each of the statements below. Based on what you read from pages A36–A47 of your science book, mark the statements which are correct by putting a ✓ mark beside the statement. If the statement is incorrect, put an X.

_____ 1.   Insects are the largest group of animals.
_____ 2.   Grasshoppers, crickets, and dragonflies have a four stage life cycle.
_____ 3.   Amphibians are animals that live part of their lives on land and part in the water.
_____ 4.   Fish need oxygen to live.
_____ 5.   Mammal mothers produce water to feed to their babies.
_____ 6.   Spiders belong to the animal group arachnids.
_____ 7.   Spiders and insects have bones.
_____ 8.   The pupa is part of a butterfly's life cycle.
_____ 9.   Gills are used by fish to get oxygen out of the water.
_____ 10.   A frog is a tadpole before it becomes an egg.
_____ 11.   Mammals have backbones and fur or hair.
_____ 12.   Whiskers are used by mammals to feel things around them.
_____ 13.   All mammals have only one baby at a time.

Part B

Directions: Use the concept bank below to complete the graphic organizer. You may want to refer to your textbook (pages A36–A47) for help. The words in the concept bank with ( ) show how many times that detail will be used in the graphic organizer. For instance, "butterfly" is followed by (2), so you would use it two times in the graphic organizer.

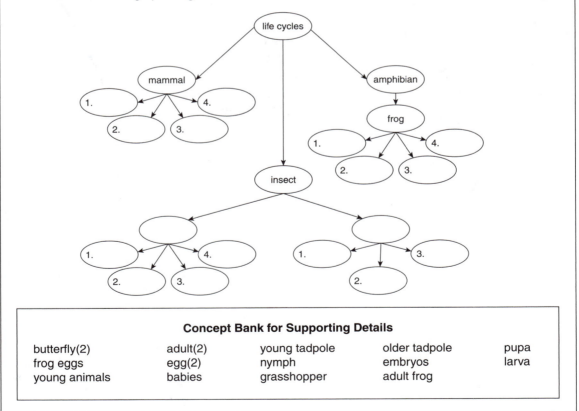

Concept Bank for Supporting Details

butterfly(2)	adult(2)	young tadpole	older tadpole	pupa
frog eggs	egg(2)	nymph	embryos	larva
young animals	babies	grasshopper	adult frog	

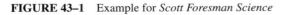

FIGURE 43–1   Example for *Scott Foresman Science*

Helping Hand for Summarizing Main Ideas and Supporting Details

Directions: Write a main idea or overall summary statement about the life cycle of insects that we have read about on pages A38–A39 from Scott Foresman Science. Write the main idea on the palm of the hand. Then write four supporting details about the butterfly's life cycle on the thumb and the fingers. Refer to your book to help you summarize the key information.

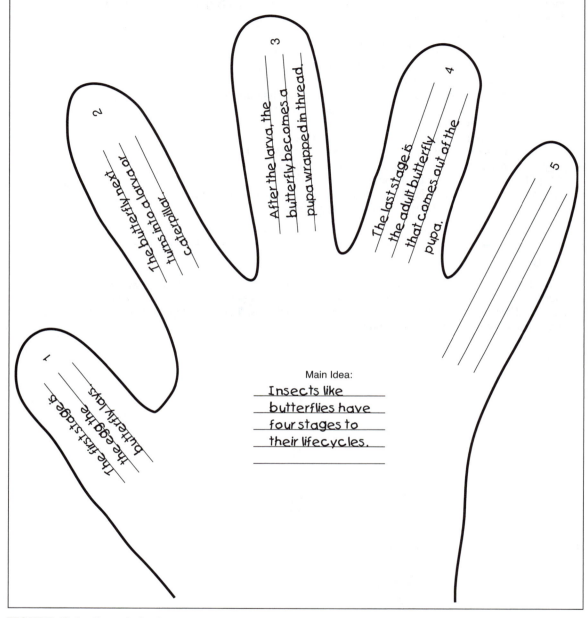

Main Idea:
Insects like
butterflies have
four stages to
their lifecycles.

2
The butterfly next
turns into a larva or
caterpillar

3
After the larva, the
butterfly becomes a
pupa wrapped in thread.

4
The last stage is
the adult butterfly
that comes out of the
pupa.

5

1
The first stage is
the egg the
butterfly lays.

FIGURE 43–2   Example for *Scott Foresman Science*

hand would work to aid learning to perceive main idea-detail organization. In this example, a superordinate concept is written in the palm of the helping hand, and subordinate ideas are recorded on the finger of the hand. As indicated in the previous procedural step, helping hands can serve as prewriting outlines to aid students in constructing summary paragraphs with a topic sentence containing a main idea followed by supportive details. In the case of the information from *Scott Foresman Science*, students would create several helping hands for such main ideas as "mammal," "amphibian," and "insect."

Further Reading

Baker, R. (1977). The effects of informational organizers on learning and retention, content knowledge, and term relationships in ninth grade social studies. In H. L. Herber & R.T. Vacca (Eds.), *Research in reading in the content areas: Third report* (pp. 148–149). Syracuse, NY: Syracuse University Reading and Language Arts Center.

Brozo, W. G., & Simpson, M. L. (1999). *Teachers, readers, learners: Expanding literacy across the content areas* (3rd ed.). Columbus, OH: Prentice Hall.

Gipe, J. P. (2006). *Multiple paths to literacy: Assessment and differentiated instruction for diverse learners, K–12* (6th ed.). Upper Saddle River, NJ: Merrill/Prentice Hall.

Roe, B. D., & Smith S. H. (2005). *Teaching reading in today's middle schools*. Boston: Houghton Mifflin.

Roe, B. D., Stoodt, B. D., & Burns, P. C. (2001). *Secondary school literacy instruction: The content areas* (7th ed.). Boston: Houghton Mifflin.

Tierney, R. J., & Readence, J. E. (2000). *Reading strategies and practice: A compendium* (5th ed.). Boston: Allyn & Bacon.

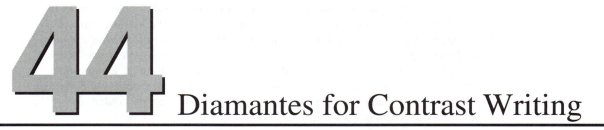

Diamantes for Contrast Writing

Strategy at a Glance: *Grade Levels 2–8*			
When to Use	**Grouping**	**Literature Type**	**Skill Areas**
○ before reading	● individual	● narrative	○ word recognition
○ during reading	● small group	● expository	● vocabulary
● after reading	● whole class		● comprehension
	○ center		● writing

Purpose

To provide students a framework or structure to follow as they contrast two story characters, real people, places, events, or concepts previously read or studied

Literature Used

Stone Fox, by John Reynolds Gardiner
A Man For All Seasons, by Robert Bolt

When to Use

After reading

Description of Strategy

A diamante (dee ah MAHN tee) is a poem shaped in the form of a diamond consisting of seven lines. This poetic form will aid students in comprehending differences and provide a structure for organizing two contrasting characters from stories, people from history, places, events, or concepts. Thus, diamantes work well whether students are writing about narrative or expository text that they have encountered. An added benefit of writing diamantes is that they reinforce knowledge of formal grammar if learners have been studying parts of speech or the functions of words in written work.

Procedures for Use

1. *Before* studying *Stone Fox*, the teacher instructs the students to pay close attention to the characters and to note opposite traits that they may have. For example, students might note differences between Little Willie and Grandfather. Students should brainstorm and record these ideas for later reference as they read through the story or hear it read aloud.

2. Either *before* or *after* the story is read, the teacher explains the purpose and structure of a diamante. "When we finish reading *Stone Fox*, you will write a diamante, or a poem in the shape of a diamond, that will contrast, or show the differences, between two characters in the book. Here's how your diamante will be organized."

3. The teacher then goes over the form of the diamante and how it will contrast two characters:

   a. The first line states the name of one of the two characters.

   b. The second line has two adjectives or words that describe this character in the first line.

   c. The third line uses three verbs, or action words, that end in *-ing* and that also describe the same character.

   d. The fourth line has two nouns that give other names to the character cited in line one. These two names are followed by two nouns that are additional ways to name the second character who is the opposite, or different, from the first character. A semicolon separates the contrasting descriptions of the two characters.

   e. The fifth line contains three words, again ending in *-ing,* that tell about the opposite second character.

   f. The sixth line uses two adjectives about the opposite character.

   g. The last line now gives the name of the second character.

4. To provide further scaffolding, the teacher may want to model for the class how to write a diamante that fulfills the required structure of the poem. This example could be based on two opposite characters from a previous story the students have read.

5. Once demonstration or modeling by the teacher has occurred, students write their own diamantes that contrast two opposite characters in *Stone Fox*. Figure 44–1 illustrates one student's diamante contrasting Little Willie and Grandfather. This example follows fairly faithfully the prescription for diamantes given in step 3.

6. Figure 44–2 provides a further example of a diamante that a collaborative learning group of older, eighth-grade students created *after* they had read and studied Robert Bolt's play *A Man for All Seasons*. This diamante contrasts the opposites Sir Thomas More and his enemy, Thomas Cromwell.

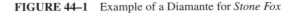

```
                    Little Willie
                  Brave, determined
              Outgoing, farming, racing
       Searchlight; Grandfather, race, sled
           Winning, intimidating, caring
                   Cold, statue-like
                      Stone Fox
```

FIGURE 44–1   Example of a Diamante for *Stone Fox*

Sir Thomas More
Compassionate, courageous
Nurturing, forgiving, encouraging
Nobleman, martyr; flatterer, bully
Climbing, lying, spying
Dangerous, insincere
Thomas Crowell

FIGURE 44–2   Example of a Diamante for *A Man for All Seasons*

Further Reading

Combs, M. (2006). *Readers and writers in primary grades: A balanced and integrated approach, K–4* (3rd ed.). Upper Saddle River, NJ: Merrill/Prentice Hall.

Sampson, M. B., Rasinski, T. V., & Sampson, M. (2003). *Total literacy: Reading, writing, and learning* (3rd ed.). Belmont, CA: Wadsworth/Thomson.

Tempke, C., Martinez, M., Yokota, J., & Naylor, A. (2002). *Children's books in children's hands: An introduction to their literature* (2nd ed.). Boston: Allyn & Bacon.

Tompkins, G. E. (2005). *Language arts: Patterns of practice* (6th ed.). Upper Saddle River, NJ: Merrill/Prentice Hall.

Tompkins, G. E. (2006). *Literacy for the 21st century: A balanced approach* (4th ed.). Upper Saddle River, NJ: Merrill/Prentice Hall.

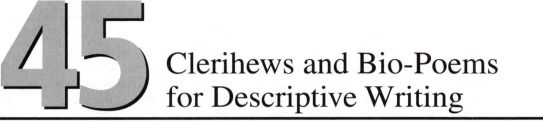

Clerihews and Bio-Poems for Descriptive Writing

EL Beneficial when working with English learners

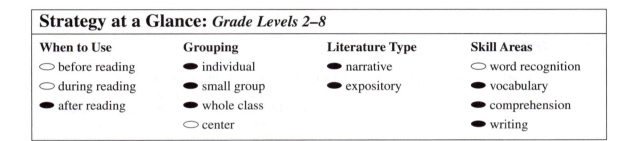

Strategy at a Glance: *Grade Levels 2–8*

When to Use	Grouping	Literature Type	Skill Areas
○ before reading	● individual	● narrative	○ word recognition
○ during reading	● small group	● expository	● vocabulary
● after reading	● whole class		● comprehension
	○ center		● writing

Purpose

To give students a framework or structure to follow as they summarize details about people, events, or things previously read or studied

Literature Used

South Carolina: Its History and Geography, by Paul Horne, Jr.

Charlie and the Chocolate Factory, by Roald Dahl, Jr.

When to Use

After reading

Description of Strategy

Like list poems, five senses poems, and diamante (see Strategies 38 and 49, respectively), both Clerihews and bio-poems offer writers a framework around which to organize their details for a description or summary of someone or something from a topic previously studied or a text previously read. The reading may be narrative or expository.

Clerihews are poems of four lines and are named after the British detective writer Edmund Clerihew Bentley, the inventor of the form. Originally lighthearted poetry about the famous, Clerihews may be on any topic: storybook characters, people from history, places in geography, scientific concepts, animals, or personal descriptions of students themselves. The form

154   Writing

consists of four lines with the first two a rhyming couplet and the last two a rhyming couplet. The first line should state the name of the person, place, animal, or concept being described. The following procedures give the requirements for the remaining three lines.

Bio-poems provide students a more extended structure than Clerihews in the form of a prescription to follow for what each line should contain. The poem may be longer or shorter, depending upon the ability levels of the students or the teacher's purpose in prescribing the content of the lines. Bio-poems are unrhymed and are usually autobiographical descriptions of the students themselves, but like Clerihews they may be on any topic studied or read about in any school subject.

Procedures for Use

1. *After* reading and studying about various towns and communities in *South Carolina: Its History and Geography,* a third-grade teacher and her students decided to write Clerihews about their local city of Rock Hill, South Carolina. In preparation for the students to write, the teacher explained that the purpose of the Clerihews was to describe the home town where the students live. Students were directed to think about details and characteristics of Rock Hill from which they could select to include in their poems.

2. The teacher then explained the form of the Clerihew. The first line should be the name of the city, Rock Hill. The second line should rhyme with the first and have a detail about the city. The third and fourth lines should rhyme and contain additional details.

3. Figure 45–1 illustrates a Clerihew that one student wrote describing the traffic congestion in Rock Hill.

4. For teachers who want greater elaboration in student writing, the following pattern or prescription shows the usual details included in each line of a bio-poem of personal description:

   Line 1—First name

   Line 2—Three or four words that describe you

   Line 3—Relative (brother, son, sister, daughter) of

   Line 4—Admirer of (three things or people)

   Line 5—Who feels (three items)

   Line 6—Who needs (three items)

   Line 7—Who fears (three items)

   Line 8—Who gives (three items)

   Line 9—Who would like to see (three items)

   Line 10—Resident of (address)

   Line 11—Last name

5. This prescription may be altered by adding other lines deemed important by the teacher (or students) or by subtracting lines. Figure 45–2 shows a teacher's modification of the pattern given in step 4 above.

6. Teachers may shift the autobiographical nature of the line requirements of bio-poems so that the writing focuses on a descriptive summary of a character, place, event, thing, or concept studied in a subject area. Figure 45–3 is an example of a bio-poem in which a fourth grader has written a thumbnail character sketch of Charlie Bucket in Roald Dahl's *Charlie and the Chocolate Factory.*

Rock Hill,
A place to chill.
With so much traffic to survive,
How do the people stay alive?

FIGURE 45–1   Example of a Clerihew

_____

(First name)

_____

(Three words that describe you)

_____

(Daughter/son of)

Who likes _____

Who feels sad when _____ and

Happy when _____

Who needs _____

Who gives _____

Who fears _____

Who would like to see _____

_____

_____

(City, State where you live)

_____

(Last name)

FIGURE 45–2   Example of a Bio-Poem as a Student Autobiography

---

Charlie
Beloved, hungry, honest, kind
Son of Mr. And Mrs. Bucket
Who loves chocolate and Grandpa Joe
Who feels lucky, excited, and grateful
Who needs food, a bed, a bigger house
Who fears losing the Grand Prize
Who wants to see the Wonka Chocolate Factory
Resident of a small house on the edge of town
Bucket

FIGURE 45–3   Example of Character Analysis Bio-Poem
for _Charlie and the Chocolate Factory_

Further Reading

Combs, M. (2006). *Readers and writers in primary grades: A balanced and integrated approach, K–4* (3rd ed.). Upper Saddle River, NJ: Merrill/Prentice Hall.

Strickland, D. S., Galda, L., & Cullinan, B. E. (2004). *Language arts: Teaching and learning.* Belmont, CA: Wadsworth/Thomson Learning.

Tompkins, G. E. (2005). *Language arts: Patterns of practice* (6th ed.). Upper Saddle River, NJ: Merrill/Prentice Hall.

Vacca, R. T., & Vacca, J. A. L. (2005). *Content area reading: Literacy and learning across the curriculum* (8th ed.). Boston: Allyn & Bacon.

46 Letter Writing

Beneficial when working with English learners

Strategy at a Glance: *Grade Levels 4–8*

When to Use	Grouping	Literature Type	Skill Areas
○ before reading	● individual	● narrative	○ word recognition
● during reading	○ small group	● expository	○ vocabulary
● after reading	○ whole class		● comprehension
	○ center		● writing

Purpose

To use descriptive writing to improve understanding of such topics as people, places, animals, and other subjects that students encounter in narrative or expository text

Literature Used

Crispin: The Cross of Lead, by AVI

When to Use

During or after reading

Description of Strategy

During or *after* reading a narrative or expository passage, students write a letter describing a person, place, thing, or animal related to the reading. Students couch their descriptions in the form of a letter to a friend, teacher, community member, story character, person from history, or any interested party. Letter writing of this sort requires learners to focus on an audience and to provide accurate information in their descriptions.

Procedures for Use

1. In a study of the Middle Ages, a sixth-grade world history teacher used AVI's novel *Crispin: The Cross of Lead* as a parallel to the chapter in the social studies book.

2. As a writing-to-learn activity, the students were to send a letter to one of the characters in the novel and describe a facet of contemporary life that would contrast to an aspect of life at the time of the Black Death in medieval England.

3. One student chose to write to the main character, Crispin, and to describe the differences between a fast food restaurant and the Green Man tavern in the medieval city of Great Wexly. The following is this writer's finished letter:

   October 25, 2010

   Dear Crispin,

   Now that your adventures are over, I hope your life is easier than it was at the beginning of the story. You went through a lot as a serf at the manor house. You had many adventures as a "wolf's head" or outlaw when anybody could kill you, no questions asked.

   Anyway, I wanted to tell you about the kinds of places we have to eat where I live in this modern world. They are a lot different from the Green Man tavern where you stayed with Bear in Great Wexly.

   At my favorite fast food place, we have a clean floor. We have clean tables to eat off of. They are not like your trestle tables and benches. Your floor of thick wooden boards was covered with dirty rushes or plants. Fleas and rats live there, and dirty dogs and pigs get to come in and sniff around. My dog Shorty gets to come in at home and sniff around under the table.

   Our food is soft drinks and hamburgers. Widow Daventry serves ales and wine to her customers. She sells bread for a penny. Wine costs a penny, too. My hamburger, drink, and fries cost my dad over four dollars. The widow has a big piece of meat that hangs from her kitchen ceiling and it's covered with flies. I haven't seen this at McDonald's.

   I enjoyed writing my letter to you. Catch you later.

   Your friend,

   Rollie Jones

4. The teacher may want to bind class letters together that come from a single unit of study like this one on *Crispin* and the Middle Ages. These can accordingly become a publication for sharing with classmates.

Further Reading

Allan, K. K., & Miller, M. S. (2005). *Literacy and learning in the content areas: Strategies for middle and secondary school teachers* (2nd ed.). New York: Houghton Mifflin.

Tompkins, G. E. (2005). *Language arts: Patterns of practice* (6th ed.). Upper Saddle River, NJ: Merrill/Prentice Hall.

Vacca, R. T., & Vacca, J. A. L. (2005). *Content area reading: Literacy and learning across the curriculum* (8th ed.). New York: Allyn & Bacon.

PART VI

Listening and Speaking Strategies

Some students experience learning difficulties because of inadequate oral language facility. One reason for this occurrence may be that the language required for listening and speaking at home does not match the language used in schools. As students transition from home to school, problems in learning may result. The final part of this text offers four strategies that emphasize the development of more proficient oral language. As with other sections, the strategies illustrated here are part of an integrated approach to teaching the five language arts so that listening, speaking, reading, writing, and viewing become mutually supportive of one another. The beginning of Part V, Writing Strategies, on pages 121–122 further discusses the integral relationship of these competencies.

If teachers delve into some of the sources cited at the end of the strategies in this section, they will find numerous concerns about appropriate and effective instruction for English learners, or ELs. In addition to the strategies discussed here, the matrix on the inside front cover indicates strategies especially useful for these students in the areas of word recognition, vocabulary, comprehension, and writing.

Some explanation is in order concerning the term "English learner." Not everyone uses this term to categorize students whose mother tongue is a language other than English but who are in settings where English is the primary mode of expressing and receiving communication, whether for everyday or academic purposes. Some other expressions commonly associated with English learners are "English as a second language" (ESOL), "English language learners" (ELLs), and "limited English proficient" (LEP). The last one includes minority dialect speakers of English as well as students for whom English is a language being acquired in addition to their native language. The emphasis throughout this text, however, is on instructing students who are growing in their competencies in any of the five language arts, whether or not English is their first language.

In instructing English learners, no matter what the label, teachers must assist them in gaining language arts proficiency in two areas: communication for basic interpersonal purposes and communication for success in academic contexts. The term for the first is "basic interpersonal communication skills" (BICS), whereas the second is "cognitive academic language proficiency skills" (CALPS). Again, a review of the sources for further reading at the end of each of the strategies for this section will provide more information about these two aspects of language development for English learners. In either area, teachers need to provide scaffolding and sheltered instruction. Although not exactly the same, both are instructional means to foster learning. They encompass, but are not limited to, the following considerations:

1. visual presentation through pictures or other graphics including graphic organizers to display information;
2. hands-on or tactile and kinesthetic learning when possible;
3. drawing on the background of learners and shared experiences either provided or activated by the teacher;

4. direct, explicit instruction that uses demonstration and modeling followed by guided and independent practice;
5. identification and teaching of pertinent vocabulary, especially *before* learning, and frequent reinforcement *during* and *after* learning so that students have multiple exposure to words and their meanings;
6. frequent monitoring of student learning by the teacher to check for understanding;
7. interaction among students and between them and the teacher so that listening and speaking are used often;
8. clearly identifiable learning goals and objectives to which the teacher regularly refers throughout a lesson;
9. continuous and on-going assessment, both formal and informal, of student progress.

Teachers who read this list will likely think, "Well, this is just good instruction," and they will be correct. Part I, Creating Successful Literacy Lessons, makes many of the same points. (See pages 1–6.) Teaching students to communicate in the language of instruction and the broader society in which they live is a challenging but not impossible task. The strategies presented here and throughout this book will help teachers accomplish this mission.

Conversational Puppets

EL Beneficial when working with English learners

Purpose

To enable students to develop comprehension through retelling a story with puppets.

Literature Used

Lon Po Po: A Red Riding Hood Story from China, by Ed Young

When to Use

After reading

Description of Strategy

Some students may be hesitant to retell a story, especially if they are learning English as a second language. This strategy offers sheltered instruction for such learners by giving them opportunities to listen to a story and retell the events and create dialogue through character puppets. The teacher may suggest a stage for a puppet play by turning a table on its side or by hanging a sheet between the backs of two chairs. (See Figure 47–1.) Shy students may hide behind the stage and hold up their puppets for the rest of the class to see as the story unfolds during the retelling. The strategy will aid in the growth of conversation skills of oral language and support reading and writing development.

Procedures for Use

1. The teacher selects a story that does not have too many characters for students to keep up with. Three to seven seems an appropriate number as in *Lon Po Po.*
2. Since *Lon Po Po* is a variant of Little Red Riding Hood stories told around the world, the teacher should activate background knowledge of such stories because some students in

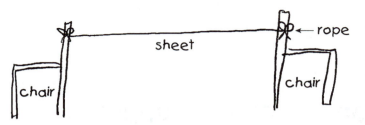

Teachers may wish to drape a sheet over the rope tied between two chairs for the children to "hide" behind. Puppets are raised up over the sheet for the audience to see.

FIGURE 47–1

the class may already be familiar with another version. The teacher may display another picture book showing an illustration of the main character and have students talk about any parts of the story with which they are familiar.

3. The teacher may then show the book cover of *Lon Po Po* or one its pictures and explain that it is another version of a story about Little Red Riding Hood and that this version comes from China. A globe or map will be helpful so that students may find the location of China.

4. Asking that the class listen to the story *during* reading it aloud, the teacher can give learners a meaningful purpose by instructing them to note how *Lon Po Po* is both alike and different from some of the stories about Little Red Riding Hood which students already know. If the teacher is reading aloud to a large group or whole class, an Elmo will be useful so that the students may more readily see the pictures and track the printed text of the book. *During* reading, English learners will find the experience helpful if the teacher stops and points to characters and objects—such as the three girls, the house, the basket, the tree—in the illustrations to enhance vocabulary and comprehension development. Having the names of objects and characters recorded somewhere in the classroom for students to see as sight words is also beneficial.

5. *After* students hear the story, discussion should occur, again with a list of the characters and significant objects recorded for everyone to see. These are the old grandmother wolf, or Lon Po Po; the mother; Shang, the oldest girl in the family; Tao, the middle child; Paotze, the youngest; and the real Po Po, or grandmother. As the discussion unfolds, pictures in the story should be revisited to remind students of the characters and to aid in remembering any needed vocabulary for a later retelling. The teacher guides the discussion by asking about the importance of story parts such as the house, the tree, the rope, and the basket.

6. Once the teacher feels satisfied that students have retained information about the characters, important story parts, and sufficient language skills, the participants can now practice with one another in retelling the story and using description and dialogue. During this phase, if any difficulties arise in recalling characters or significant story parts, the teacher should encourage students to return to the book and the recorded names and objects as aids to memory and language. The goal for students is not perfect oral language but for them to have enough facility in the retelling to communicate the story adequately to other listeners.

7. Puppets will also serve as an aid to recalling the story. Participants can construct either paper bag or stick puppets to represent the characters and to be used in retelling the story behind the stage. (Figure 47–2 offers suggestions for making such props.) With teacher guidance, English learners with more intermediate and advanced language skills could write scripts for a puppet play or for use in conjunction with a readers' theater production of the story. (See pages 93–94 on readers' theater as a strategy for language development.) Whether reading from a script or doing an unscripted, more spontaneous retelling, English learners will gain confidence in using oral language with puppets as props.

FIGURE 47–2

8. As an additional consideration, teachers may want to place a copy of the storybook, laminated cards with objects and character names printed on them, and the puppets in a learning center for students to do multiple retellings for independent practice.

Alternate Idea

This strategy works well for subject areas when students are learning about people who have made significant historical contributions, such as George Washington in social studies, Sir Isaac Newton in science, or Georgia O'Keefe in art. Children's literature abounds with biographies. Story retellings based on such people in history will develop knowledge of academic content.

Further Reading

Coleman, R., & Goldenberg, C. (2009). What does research say about effective practices for English learners? Introduction and part I: Oral language proficiency. *Kappa Delta Pi Record, 46,* 10–16.

Coody, B. (1997). *Using literature with young children* (5th ed.). Madison, WI: Brown & Benchmark.

Keifer, B., Hepler, S., & Hickman, J. (2007). *Charlotte Huck's children's literature* (9th ed.). Boston: McGraw Hill.

Lessow-Hurley, J. (2003). *Meeting the needs of second language learners.* Alexandria, VA: Association for Supervision and Curriculum Development.

National Council of Teachers of English (2006). *NCTE position paper on the role of English teachers in Educating English language learners (ELLs).* Retrieved October 24, 2007, from http://www.ncte.org/about/over/positions/category/div/124545.htm.

Norton, D. E., & Norton, S. E. (2003). *Through the eyes of a child: An introduction to children's literature* (6th ed.). Upper Saddle River, NJ: Merrill/Prentice Hall.

Opitz, M. F., & Guccione, L. M. (2009). *Comprehension and English language learners: 25 oral reading strategies that cross proficiency levels.* Portsmouth, NH: Heinemann.

Raines, S. C., & Canady, R. J. (1989). *Story s-t-r-e-t-c-h-e-r-s: Activities to expand children's favorite books.* Mt. Rainier, MD: Gryphon House.

48 Directed Listening-Thinking Activity (DL-TA)—With T-Chart

(EL) Beneficial when working with English learners

Strategy at a Glance: *Grade Levels All*

When to Use	Grouping	Literature Type	Skill Areas
● before reading	○ individual	● narrative	○ word recognition
● during reading	● small group	● expository	● vocabulary
● after reading	● whole class		● comprehension
	○ center		○ writing

Purpose

To foster active listening, encourage speaking through oral responses, and engage in higher-level thinking.

Literature Used

Pet Show! by Ezra Jack Keats

When to Use

Before, during, and after reading

Description of Strategy

This strategy focuses on learners' active listening to segments of a selection read aloud by the teacher, their responses to higher-level questions that call for hypothesizing about upcoming events or information, and their continued listening, as another segment is read aloud, to confirm whether their predictions were correct. This process repeats itself for several rounds until the selection is completed.

Procedures for Use

1. The teacher chooses a selection that is new to the listeners. It should be unfamiliar so that, when students predict what will happen next in a narrative passage, or what new information an expository will convey, their hypotheses are not derived from previous knowledge of the text.

2. *Pet Show!* is a picture book. The teacher should ideally use a paperback version of *Pet Show!* because the cover includes not only the title but also an attractive illustration. If only hardback is available, the teacher can begin by holding up the first double-page spread, which is virtually the same as the paperback cover but which also has the opening sentence of the story. *Before* reading, the teacher will try to arouse curiosity about the story by saying "This book is about pets" and ask such questions as "Do any of you have a pet? Is it an inside or outside pet? Has it ever been in a show?"

   Also *before* reading, the teacher should engage students with the book's title and cover features and thus build background for the reading aloud that is to follow. The teacher should draw attention to the cover art and title, discuss these, and encourage learners to guess what the story will be about. Thought-provoking questions at this stage will aid with students formulating initial hypotheses. Here are some suggested opening questions that the teacher might pose:

   > What are the boys and girls on the cover of this book doing?
   >
   > What do you think the sign says? (The teacher should read the sign aloud and discuss it if no one responds.)
   >
   > Do you think the children on the cover of the book have pets?
   >
   > The cover says 'Prizes.' What do you think that means?
   >
   > What kind of pet show do you think the sign is talking about or advertising?
   >
   > Are the children on the cover of the book interested in going to the pet show? Why do you think so?

3. *During* reading the story aloud, the teacher will pause at a predetermined place and give the listeners a chance to discuss whether their initial predictions occurred. At this point, the teacher also elicits new guesses about what will happen next as a result of what has occurred so far in the plot. If students seem stuck in formulating predictions, the teacher might offer sheltered instruction through cues and prompts like the following:

   > What do you think Archie will do when he can't find his cat?
   >
   > Which pet do you think the judges will choose to win the prize? Why?
   >
   > After the nice lady wins the prize for 'the cat with the longest whiskers,' what do you think Archie will do? Is this cat really her cat or someone else's?

   Once students have finished this second round of hypotheses, the teacher continues to read aloud another segment of the book. This round might be the last one for a short book like *Pet Show!* If the text is longer, other rounds of predictions may follow until the conclusion of the selection. Everything depends on how the teacher wants to segment the text.

4. *After* reading, when the teacher concludes the story, listeners confirm or reject their final round of predictions and offer explanations based on the story. Final listening comprehension questions for *Pet Show!* that encourage students to operate at deeper levels of understanding might concern whether they believe Archie made a good decision about the "nice" lady's ribbon or why the judges awarded a prize to all the pet show participants. The teacher might also ask students whether their guesses about what would happen were influenced by the predictions of other class members.

5. Variations on the DL-TA exist such as the directed reading-thinking activity (DR-TA). Some of the resources in Further Reading describe these. The strategy discussed here, however, focuses on scaffolding classroom instruction to help English learners become active in listening and to develop facility in discussing their ideas in a group or class setting.

Alternate Idea

A T-chart is a helpful graphic organizer that provides further scaffolding with the DL-TA. As Figure 48–1 illustrates, the teacher records in the left column student predictions about what will

T-Chart	
Before Listening Predictions	True or Revised Predictions *After* Listening
All the children will take a pet to the show.	True
The boys and girls will bring their dogs and cats.	Some brought a parrot, fishes, a frog, a canary, ants, a mouse, a turtle, and many more pets.
Archie will let the nice lady keep the ribbon.	True

FIGURE 48–1　T-Chart Example for *Pet Show!*

happen *before* they listen to a passage. Then as the students hear the segment read aloud, they have an opportunity to determine whether their hypotheses were true or to revise them based on the new information heard *after* they have listened to the teacher finish reading aloud the next segment of the story.

Further Reading

Anderson, N. A. (2010). *Elementary children's literature: Infancy through age 13* (3rd ed.). Boston: Allyn & Bacon.

Carrier, K. A. (2005). Key issues for teaching English language learners in academic classrooms. *Middle School Journal, 37*(2), 4–9.

Coleman, R., & Goldenberg, C. (2009). What does research say about effective practices for English learners? Introduction and part I: Oral language proficiency. *Kappa Delta Pi Record, 46*, 10–16.

Gunning, T. (2005). *Creating literacy instruction for all students* (5th ed.). Boston: Allyn & Bacon.

Johns, J., & Lenski, S. D. (2001). *Improving reading: Strategies and resources* (3rd ed.). Dubuque, IA: Kendall/Hunt.

National Council of Teachers of English (2006). *NCTE position paper on the role of English teachers in educating English language learners (ELLs)*. Retrieved October 24, 2007, from http://www.ncte.org/about/over/positions/category/div/124545.htm.

Rubin, D. (2002). *Diagnosis and correction in reading instruction* (4th ed.). Boston: Allyn & Bacon.

Tompkins, G. E. (2005). *Language arts: Patterns of practice* (6th ed.). Upper Saddle River, NJ: Merrill/Prentice Hall.

Vacca, R. T., & Vacca, J. A. L. (2005). *Content area reading: Literacy and learning across the curriculum* (8th ed.). Boston: Allyn & Bacon.

49 Echo Reading

EL Beneficial when working with English learners

Strategy at a Glance: *Grade Levels All*

When to Use	Grouping	Literature Type	Skill Areas
● before reading	○ individual	● narrative	● word recognition
● during reading	● small group	○ expository	● vocabulary
○ after reading	● whole class		○ comprehension
	○ center		○ writing

Purpose

To facilitate listening and speaking and to aid in reading fluency through the development of language competencies such as phonics principles, sight word recognition, appropriate phrasing, syntactic patterns, and the conventions of punctuation

Literature Used

The ABC Bunny, by Wanda Gág

Drummer Hoff, adapted by Barbara Emberly

Goodnight Moon, by Margaret Wise Brown

The House in the Night, by Susan Marie Swanson

"If All the Seas Were One Sea," from *The Real Mother Goose,* compiled and illustrated by Blanche Fisher Wright

Is Your Mama a Llama? by Deborah Guarino

Rosie's Walk, by Pat Hutchins

Tortillas and Lullabies/Tortillas y cancioncitas, by Lynn Reiser

Who Sank the Boat? by Pamela Allen

When to Use

Before and during reading

Description of Strategy

Echo reading is a form of imitative reading and often suggested as a way to structure choral reading in the classroom. Echo reading is also an easy and enjoyable way of developing many important language competencies, depending on the needs of learners. The basic idea is that a skilled reader, such as the teacher or another student, reads aloud a short segment of text as others listen and then repeat it orally by mimicking the phrasing. Pairs of students, small groups, or a whole class may participate in echo reading.

The teacher should select literature that is predictable and repetitive. Books may be predictable and repetitive in different and sometimes overlapping ways from micro- to macro-language skills. Some books like *Goodnight Moon* and *The ABC Bunny* have text that illustrates language principles for phonics and for spelling patterns. *Goodnight Moon* repeats /oo/ in "moon"; in the second, accented syllable of "balloon"; and in "room." It also has many rhyming or spelling patterns in words such as "socks" and "clocks." Awareness of phonograms like "-ocks" in these words will help learners with pronunciation when they encounter others with the same pattern. The same idea holds true for *The ABC Bunny* as is illustrated by the phonogram "-ash" in the rhyming triplet "flash," "dash," and "crash." If students need help with how sounds in words are alike and different, teachers can look for other examples like these, with the beginnings or the onsets of the words having different sounds while the rime or the phonogram as in "–ash" has the same sound. Teachers might use the book and instruct students to listen to lines and find words starting with the same sound as with "fat and funny" for the letter "F".

Besides repeating sounds, both *Goodnight Moon* and *The ABC Bunny* repeat many of the same words and thereby aid in reinforcing sight words for students through multiple exposures. Examples include "moon" in the first book and "bunny" in the second. At the level of word repetition, *Drummer Hoff* might be an even better choice. In addition to having many phonograms in its rhyming words, the book repeats many times words like "brought," "fired," and "off."

For teachers who want to help students with language components larger than sounds and words, some books are predictable at the syntactic level or in their arrangement of words into meaningful units. A good example is *Rosie's Walk*. The book is one sentence, but most of the text is a series of prepositional phrases such as "around the pond" indicating where Rosie the hen goes on her walk. Although prepositions are difficult to define in abstract, verbal terms alone, the illustrations make the meaning of these parts of speech understandable as Rosie goes "over the haystack" or "under the beehives." English learners can act out these locational phrases as they echo them in response to the teacher.

Other books might be used to acquaint students with further components of language. Teachers could use echo reading with *Who Sank the Boat?* or *Is Your Mama a Llama?* to give students practice in grouping words into phrases and the syntactic structure of how to form questions. Both books are also strong selections for reading competencies at the micro-level of certain phonics generalizations and phonograms as already discussed. *Tortillas and Lullabies/Tortillas y cancioncitas* has such sentences as "I gathered flowers for my mother; and my doll gathered flowers for me." Besides expanding knowledge of vocabulary with words like "flowers" and "doll," the book contains sentences following the subject-verb-object pattern. As readers echo these, teachers could use them to demonstrate this aspect of syntactic order.

For more advanced English learners, the traditional Mother Goose ditty "If All the Seas Were One Sea" shows how to form the structure of conditional dependent clauses beginning with "if." Because this clause is introductory throughout the poem and, therefore, is followed by a comma, it also illustrates a convention of punctuation as in these two lines:

If all the trees were one tree,

What a great tree that would be!

This rhyming couplet and all the others end in an exclamation point. As part of echo reading, the teacher could instruct students that this punctuation mark indicates emotion and that they should read the lines with a lot of feeling.

The point is that echo reading has numerous possibilities to promote understanding about various facets of language. It all depends on the needs of the learners and the aim of the teacher. The following procedures demonstrate uses of this strategy for selected purposes.

Procedures for Use

1. If students are beginning English learners who need to increase their stock of vocabulary words and require assistance with phrasing for greater fluency, *The House in the Night* is a strong choice. Its vocabulary is particularly beneficial in developing functional word meanings for basic, everyday communication. Words included in the text are related to home, animals, time, and celestial bodies. Among these are "key," "house," "bed," "bird," "moon," "starry," "sun." All are within the written text and illustrated by the pictures. In addition, the illustrations have a dog, a cat, and kittens as pets in the house and a teddy bear as a toy. The teacher may want to focus on these words as well for vocabulary development. The pictures and written text are also useful in aiding students with important opposites like "dark" and "light." The teacher should survey the book to select which words to emphasize.

2. *Before* students engage in echo reading, a picture walk is an effective way to build important background for comprehending the selected vocabulary. (See pages 91–92 for a fuller discussion of picture walk.) If the classroom has an Elmo, the teacher can project the illustrations to make them bigger so that a larger group of students may more readily see them and the words in the text. For instance, in previewing the word "moon," the teacher can show a picture of the moon and point out the phrase "Through the dark glows the moon" at the same time calling attention to the word in the text. This double-page spread in the middle of the book can be contrasted with the illustration near the beginning which shows a bed and glowing lamp through an open door and contains the phrase "In that light rests a bed." In this way, teachers can use the two parts of the book and point out the difference between the antonyms "light" and "dark."

3. Once the survey of important words is completed and adequate schema provided through a picture walk, the teacher can begin the echo reading. Before engaging students in the strategy, the teacher will want to demonstrate how the procedure works. Using the opening sentence, the teacher should model the process by orally reading "Here is the key to the house" and instruct students to then mimic the line by repeating it.

4. Our experience with students, whether English is their first or second language, shows that they may be somewhat reluctant to echo the lines. A lot of encouragement as well as cuing and prompting with appropriate phrasing, volume, intonation, and cadence with the phrasing may be needed at this point. There may also be a need for several repetitions before students overcome their hesitancy to participate actively. The teacher should carefully monitor student engagement and phrasing.

5. An advantage to echo reading with *The House in the Night* and with other literature is that it may occur multiple times with the same book for the same learning outcomes if they require reinforcement for students. The same book may also be used for different learning aims. If the teacher decides that English learners would benefit from work with prepositions and prepositional phrases, *The House in the Night* is an excellent selection for that purpose because these grammatical forms are on each page containing written text. Again, the prepositions and phrases should be previewed and discussed through a picture walk *before* echo reading. If students need help with demonstrative pronouns like "that," echo reading of *The House in the Night* also could assist in teaching this aspect of everyday communication. Although the demonstrative pronoun "this" is not in the text, the teacher could discuss its use and meaning during the picture walk by contrasting "this" with the word "that" when the latter appears in the text.

Further Reading

Brown, D. H. (2007). *Teaching by principles: An interactive approach to language pedagogy* (3rd ed.). White Plains, NY: Pearson.

Center on Instruction (2006). *Research-based recommendations for instruction and academic interventions: Practical guidelines for the education of English language learners: Book 1of 3.* Retrieved July 20, 2010, from www.centeroninstruction.org.

Center on Instruction (2006). *Research-based recommendations for serving adolescent newcomers: Practical guidelines for the education of English language learners: Book 2 of 3.* Retrieved July 20, 2010, from www.centeroninstruction.org.

Coleman, R., & Goldenberg, C. (2009). What does research say about effective practices for English learners? Introduction and part I: Oral language proficiency. *Kappa Delta Pi Record 46,* 10–16.

Harris, A. J., & Sipay, E. R. (1990). *How to increase reading ability: A guide to developmental and remedial methods* (9th ed.). New York: Longman.

Johns, J., & Lenski, S. D. (2001). *Improving reading methods: Strategies and resources* (3rd ed.). Dubuque. IA: Kendall/Hunt.

National Council of Teachers of English (2006). *NCTE position paper on the role of English teachers in educating English language learners (ELLs).* Retrieved October 24, 2007, from http://www. ncte.org/about/over/positions/category/div/124545.htm.

Opitz, M. F., & Guccione, L. M. (2009). *Comprehension and English language learners: 25 oral reading strategies that cross proficiency levels.* Portsmouth, NH: Heinemann.

Strickland, D. S., Galda, L., & Cullinan, B. E. (2004). *Language arts: Teaching and learning.* Belmont, CA: Wadsworth/Thomson Learning.

Tompkins, G. E. (2005). *Language arts: Patterns of practice* (6th ed.). Upper Saddle River, NJ: Merrill/Prentice Hall.

Literary Posters

EL Beneficial when working with English learners

Strategy at a Glance: *Grade Levels All*			
When to Use	**Grouping**	**Literature Type**	**Skill Areas**
○ before reading	○ individual	● narrative	● word recognition
● during reading	● small group	● expository	● vocabulary
● after reading	● whole class		● comprehension
	○ center		● writing

Purpose

To organize and summarize information into main ideas and supporting details through writing and visual representation

Literature Used

From Abenaki to Zuni: A Dictionary of Native American Tribes, by Evelyn Wolfson

When to Use

During and after reading

Description of Strategy

Integrating all the language arts of listening, speaking, reading, writing, and viewing, literary posters also develop expressive as well as receptive abilities in learners as they summarize information and insights and then share these with others. As part of *after* reading, this strategy promotes competency in word recognition, vocabulary development, and greater understanding of text as students discuss what they have read, listen to ideas presented, make decisions about important information to include on posters, and assess how best to represent it visually. Because the use of visuals fosters language development in English learners and other students, literary posters are especially helpful in this regard. The strategy seems to work best with pairs or small groups who have been assigned different topics to read and research. Students then share what they have learned about their particular topic with other class members as a means of further enhancing listening and speaking. The procedures that follow demonstrate the strategy with small groups of students in seventh grade as an *after* reading activity as part of a study of southeastern Native Americans associated with South Carolina history.

Procedures for Use

1. *Abenaki to Zuni: A Dictionary of Native American Tribes* contains short sketches of approximately two to five pages. A map near the beginning shows the location of major cultural groups of Native Americans. Using multiple copies of the book, the teacher divides the class into several small groups. Each is assigned to research a culture from what is now the southeastern United States: Catawba, Cherokee, Chickasaw, Choctaw, Creek, and Seminole. This research is part of a study of South Carolina history of the eighteenth and nineteenth centuries. Although not all of these cultures lived in what is today South Carolina, each is associated with it through interactions like trade, treaties, or conflicts with leaders like Andrew Jackson, who was born in the state.

2. The teacher provides each student group with a sheet of paper and indicates to fold it into four heavily creased sections. After unfolding these, students then draw lines onto the creases so that there are four clearly defined quarters. These will serve as a rough copy to record ideas about each group's assignment. For instance, one group may be researching the Cherokee.

3. The teacher instructs groups to select four cultural components from a predetermined list like the following: foods eaten, means of transportation, shelter type(s), clothing worn, specific geographic locations where the Native Americans lived, religious beliefs, dealings with European colonists, meaning of the Native American name (i.e., Catawba). The teacher should tell students to select from the list the four cultural features that they think are significant based upon their upcoming reading and research. Students record one cultural aspect on each quarter of their sheet of paper.

4. Students now use *From Abenaki to Zuni* and read about their assigned group of Native Americans. As they read, they decide about the details that they want to include under each subtopic in the squares on their papers. The teacher might also allow students to consult other sources of information whether online or in their social studies text or library.

5. Once students have completed their research and rough summaries on their sheets of paper, the teacher gives each group a poster board and marking pens. Again, students record their four cultural traits on their posters, but this time they write the name of their assigned Native Americans in the center. Teachers may want to consider laminating the posters beforehand and using erasable marking pens for ease in editing and polishing by students. A beginning literary poster might look this way:

Shelter Types	Religious Beliefs

Cherokee

Group's Geographic Locations	Foods Eaten

6. Students now record supportive details (as bullet points, if so desired) under each of the four headings, leaving enough room for accompanying illustrations of significant ideas. The teacher should emphasize that an important criterion for effective posters is that they present readers and viewers key information in a condensed, memorable form. This activity requires students to engage in critical thinking as they edit and polish their posters for presentation to others.

7. In illustrating their posters, students may do original drawings or go to a source like *Wikimedia* and download visuals to attach.

8. Having created their final product for presentation to other members of the class, students now share their posters. The teacher may display these around the classroom for further examination by other groups to reinforce the content studied.

Further Reading

Bear, R. E. (2010). *The value of posters.* Retrieved July 15, 2010, from http://education.jhu.edu/newhorizons/strategies/topics/literacy/articles/the-value-of-posters.

Brown, D. H. (2007). *Teaching by principles: An interactive approach to language pedagogy.* (3rd ed.). White Plains, NY: Pearson.

Carrier, K. A. (2005). Key issues for teaching English language learners in academic classrooms. *Middle School Journal, 37(2),* 4–9.

Center on Instruction (2006). *Research-based recommendations for instruction and academic interventions: Practical guidelines for the education of English language learners: Book 1 of 3.* Retrieved July 20, 2010, from www.centeroninstruction.org.

Center on Instruction (2006). *Research-based recommendations for serving adolescent newcomers: Practical guidelines for the education of English language learners: Book 2 of 3.* Retrieved July 20, 2010, from www.centeroninstruction.org.

Coleman, R., & Goldenberg, C. (2009). What does research say about effective practices for English learners? Part III: Promoting literacy development. *Kappa Delta Pi Record, 46,* 106–111.

Harry Potter character posters. Retrieved July 14, 2010, from http://www.teachervision.fen.com/harry-potter/lesson-plan.

Johnson, T. D., & Louis, D. R. (1987). *Literacy through literature.* Portsmouth, NH: Heinemann.

National Council of Teachers of English (2006). *NCTE position paper on the role of English teachers in educating English language learners (ELLs).* Retrieved October 24, 2007, from http://www.ncte.org/about/over/positions/category/div/124545.htm.

Rothenberg, C., & Fisher, D. (2007). *Teaching English language learners: A differentiated approach.* Upper Saddle River, NJ: Pearson.

Appendix:
Some Recommended Literacy Websites

Websites available today may seem overwhelming to educators. The sites listed here are easy for learners, teachers, parents, and other caregivers to navigate and will be helpful in literacy development.

About Children's Literature at *http://www.childrenslit.com*

This site reviews thousands of books each year. Features include interviews with authors and illustrators, themed reviews of books, author and illustrator links, lists of award winners, resources for parents and teachers, classroom materials, and teaching suggestions.

The American Library Association Home Page at *http://ala.org*

The American Library Association posts excellent reading lists for children and adolescents. The site contains information about authors and award-winning books, censorship, activities to use with literature, and links to related sites. For example, two good ones are "Great Web Sites for Kids" and "Sites for Parents, Teachers, and Caregivers." Listed in the first is http://www.miscositas.com, which contains online stories and virtual picture books. The second has a link to "Literacy Connections," which has information on reading, teaching, and tutoring.

Barnes and Noble Bookstore at *www.bn.com*

This commercial bookstore chain has a helpful site for teachers and parents as well as an online story time for children where featured books are read aloud either by the book's author or a celebrity. Background music and graphics add to the appeal. The site also suggests books for a variety of ages; gender-specific selections; reading levels, if a lexile score is known; series books; and academically useful books and toys for students.

The Children's Literature Web Guide at *www.ucalgary.cal/~dkbrown*

This resource provides access to literature for children and young adults, lists of award-winning and recommended books, topical bibliographies, lesson plans, information about authors and illustrators, and much more. Topical bibliographies are useful for teaching thematically.

Everything ESL: The K-12 Resource from Judie Haynes at *http://everythingESL.net*

The home page table of contents includes numerous topics that support teachers in the oral language of learners in social and academic settings. As a thirty-plus-year veteran teacher who has written for the Association of Supervision and Curriculum Development, Judie Haynes is the creator of this web site. She summarizes research on English as a second language and applies it to teaching. Teaching tips, activities, and lesson plans are available, although there is a charge for the latter. Users of this resource may print black-line graphic organizers.

National Council of Teachers of English at *http://www.ncte.org*

This organization's website provides summaries of current research. For instance, the article "English Language Learners: A Policy Brief" focuses on learners whose first language is not English. The discussion of myths that people have about English learners versus the reality is particularly informative. Besides the lengthy inclusion of these kinds of summaries and policy statements on various aspects of language, NCTE lists other useful websites.

Reading Rockets: Reading Comprehension & Language Arts Teaching . . . at *www.readingrockets.org*

An excellent compendium of resources for parents, teachers, principals, and librarians, Reading Rockets includes a brief introduction to teaching reading and classroom strategies for *before, during,* and *after* reading. An annotated website list, video clips of authors for children and adults, professional development webcasts, and videos of best practice in teaching reading are among many of its features.

ReadWriteThink at *http://www.readwritethink.org*

Under the auspices of the International Reading Association and the National Council of Teachers of English, this site is for teachers and "savvy" parents. Among its plethora of offerings, it includes lesson plans for specific objectives written by practitioners in the field of literacy; resources for specified grade levels of K, 1–3, 3–4, 5–6, 7–8, and 9–12; IRA, NCTE, and most state standards; and assessment rubrics. The site also provides opportunities to submit lesson plans.

South Carolina State Library at *http://www.statelibrary.sc.gov*

This site includes a video clip of a librarian introducing new children's books. Additional resources are books for seasonal and recreational reading, "family friendly" South Carolina standards for grades K-4 along with suggested activities to support growth in literacy skills, and a calendar that offers ideas for developing family literacy. Other resources include lists of books, suggested grade levels, ratings, and summaries, as well as suggestions for talking and thinking about recommended selections. Under the "web resources for children's services" is a link to **Carol Hurst's Children's Literature Site**, by Carol Otis Hurst and Rebecca Otis, at http://carolhurst.com. Educators directing their web finders to this recommended site will not be disappointed in the many ideas for teaching literacy through children's books. Teachers also will want to investigate the web sites of their own state libraries as potential literacy resources.

Storyline Online at *http://www.storylineonline.net*

The first screen displays attractive covers for five children's books that are featured at the time of retrieval. Once a cover is clicked, a representative of the Screen Actors Guild shows the selected book and reads it aloud as pictures of the book are shown. This resource encourages student interest in literature and helps foster automaticity if the student is directed to follow the displayed text as the actor reads it aloud. Parents and teachers may engage learners in suggested *after* reading activities to promote literacy. Sponsored by a grant from Verizon, the site is free for the clicking.

References

Allan, K. K., & Miller, M. S. (2005). Literacy and *Learning in the content areas: Strategies for middle and secondary school teachers* (2nd ed.). New York: Houghton Mifflin.

Anderson, N. A. (2010). *Elementary children's literature: Infancy through age 13* (3rd ed.). Boston: Allyn & Bacon.

Baker, R. (1977). The effects of informational organizers on learning and retention, content knowledge, and term relationships in ninth grade social studies. In H. L. Herber & R. T. Vacca (Eds.), *Research in reading in the content areas: Third report* (pp. 148–149). Syracuse, NY: Syracuse University Reading and Language Arts Center.

Bear, R. E. (2010). *The value of posters.* Retrieved July 15, 2010, from http://education.jhu.edu/newhorizons/strategies/topics/literacy/articles/the-value-of-posters.

Billmeyer, R., & Barton, M. L. (2002). *Teaching reading in the content areas: If not me, then who?* (2nd ed.). Aurora, CO: Mid-continent Research for Education and Learning.

Brown, D. H. (2007). *Teaching by principles: An interactive approach to language pedagogy* (3rd ed.). White Plains, NY: Pearson.

Brozo, W. G., & Simpson, M. L. (1999). *Teachers, readers, learners: Expanding literacy across the content areas* (3rd ed.). Upper Saddle River, NJ: Prentice Hall.

Carmine, D., Silbert, S., Kame'enui, E. J., Tarver, S. G., & Jungjohann, K. (2006). *Teaching struggling and at-risk readers: A direct instruction approach.* Columbus, OH: Merrill/Prentice Hall.

Carrier, K. A. (2005). Key issues for teaching English language learners in academic classrooms. *Middle School Journal, 37(2),* 4–9.

Center on Instruction (2006). *Research-based recommendations for instruction and academic interventions: Practical guidelines for the education of English language learners: Book 1 of 3.* Retrieved July 20, 2010, from www.centeroninstruction.org.

Center on Instruction (2006). *Research-based recommendations for serving adolescent newcomers: Practical guidelines for the education of English language learners: Book 2 of 3.* Retrieved July 20, 2010, from www.centeroninstruction.org.

Coleman, R., & Goldenberg, C. (2009). What does research say about effective practices for English learners? Introduction and part I: Oral language proficiency. *Kappa Delta Pi Record, 46,* 10–16.

Coleman, R., & Goldenberg, C. (2009). What does research say about effective practices for English learners? Part III: Promoting literacy development. *Kappa Delta Pi Record, 46,* 106–111.

Combs, M. (2006). *Readers and writers in primary grades: A balanced and integrated approach, K–4* (3rd ed.). Upper Saddle River, NJ: Merrill/Prentice Hall.

Coody, B. (1997). *Using literature with young children* (5th ed.). Madison, WI: Brown & Benchmark.

Cooper, J. D. (2000). *Literacy: Helping children construct meaning* (4th ed.). Boston: Houghton Mifflin.

Cooter, R. B., Jr., & Flynt, E. S. (1996). *Teaching reading in the content areas: Developing content literacy for all students.* Englewood Cliffs, NJ: Prentice Hall.

Cunningham, P. (2000). *Phonics they use* (3rd ed.). New York: Longman.

Cunningham, P., & Allington, R. (1994). Classrooms that work. New York: HarperCollins.

Classrooms that work. New York: HarperCollins.

Cunningham, P. M., Moore, S. A., Cunningham, J. W., & Moore, D. W. (1995). *Reading and writing in elementary classrooms: Strategies and observations* (3rd ed.). White Plains, NY: Longman.

Donelson, K. L., & Nilsen, A. P. (1997). *Literature for today's young adults* (5th ed.). New York: Addison Wesley Longman.

Fernald, G. (1943). *Remedial techniques in basic school subjects.* New York: McGraw-Hill.

Frayer, D. A., Frederick, W. C., & Klausmeier, H. J. (1969). *A schema for testing the level of concept mastery.* Technical Report No. 16. Madison, WI: University of Wisconsin Research and Development Center for Cognitive Learning.

Frey, N., & Fisher, D. (2006). *Language arts workshop: Purposeful reading and writing instruction.* Columbus, OH: Pearson Prentice Hall.

Gipe, J. P. (2006). *Multiple paths to literacy: Assessment and differentiated instruction for diverse learners, K–12* (6th ed.). Upper Saddle River, NJ: Merrill/Prentice Hall.

Graves, M., Juel, C., & Graves, B. (1998). *Teaching reading in the 21st century.* Needham Heights, MA: Allyn & Bacon.

Gunning, T. (2005). *Creating literacy instruction for all students* (5th ed.). Boston: Allyn & Bacon.

Harris, A. J., & Sipay, E. R. (1990). *How to increase reading ability: A guide to developmental and remedial methods* (9th ed.). New York: Longman.

Harry Potter character posters. Retrieved July 14, 2010, from http://www.teachervision.fen.com/harry-potter/lesson-plan.

Hopkins, L. B. (1987). *Pass the poetry, please!* New York: Harper & Row.

Johns, J., & Lenski, S. D. (2001). *Improving reading: Strategies and resources* (3rd ed.). Dubuque, IA: Kendall/Hunt.

Johnson, T. D., & Louis, D. R. (1987). *Literacy through literature.* Portsmouth, NH: Heinemann.

Keifer, B., Hepler, S., & Hickman, J. (2007). *Charlotte Huck's children's literature* (9th ed.). Boston: McGraw Hill.

Lessow-Hurley, J. (2003). *Meeting the needs of second language learners.* Alexandria, VA: Association for Supervision and Curriculum Development.

Manzo, A. V. (1969). The ReQuest procedure. *Journal of Reading, 11,* 123–126.

National Council of Teachers of English (2006). *NCTE position paper on the role of English teachers in educating English language learners (ELLs).* Retrieved October 24, 2007, from http://www.ncte.org/about/over/positions/category/div/124545.htm.

Norton, D. E., & Norton, S. E. (2003). *Through the eyes of a child: An introduction to children's literature* (6th ed.). Upper Saddle River, NJ: Merrill/Prentice Hall.

Norton, T., & Land, B. L. (1992). A multisensory approach to teaching spelling in remedial English. *Teaching English in the Two-Year College, 19,* 192–195.

Opitz, M. F., & Guccione, L. M. (2009). *Comprehension and English language learners: 25 oral reading strategies that cross proficiency levels.* Portsmouth, NH: Heinemann.

Raines, S. C., & Canady, R. J. *Story s-t-r-e-t-c-h-e-r-s: Activities to expand children's favorite books.* Mt. Ranier: Gryphon House.

Reutzel, D. R., & Cooter, R. (2000). *Teaching children to read: Putting the pieces together* (3rd ed.). Columbus, OH: Merrill.

Robinson, F. (1946). *Effective study.* New York: HarperCollins.

Roe, B. D., & Smith, S. H. (2005). *Teaching reading in today's middle schools.* Boston: Houghton Mifflin.

Roe, B. D., Stoodt, B. D., & Burns, P. C. (2001). *Secondary school literacy instruction: The content areas* (7th ed.). Boston: Houghton Mifflin.

Rothenberg, C., & Fisher, D. (2007). *Teaching English language learners: A differentiated approach.* Upper Saddle River, NJ: Pearson.

Rubin D. (2002). *Diagnosis and correction in reading instruction* (4th ed.). Boston: Allyn & Bacon.

Ruddell, R. B., & Ruddell, M. R. (1995). *Teaching children to read and write: Becoming an influential teacher.* Boston: Allyn & Bacon.

Sampson, M. B., Rasinski, T. V., & Sampson, M. (2003). *Total literacy: Reading, writing, and learning* (3rd ed.). Belmont, CA: Wadsworth/Thomson.

Strickland, D. S., Galda, L., & Cullinan, B. E. (2004). *Language arts: Teaching and learning.* Belmont, CA: Wadsworth/Thomson Learning.

Taylor, B., Harris, L. A., Pearson, P. D., & Garcia, G. (1995). *Reading difficulties: Instruction and assessment* (2nd ed.). New York: McGraw-Hill.

Tempke, C., Martinez, M., Yokota, J., & Naylor, A. (2002). *Children's books in children's hands: An introduction to their literature* (2nd ed.) Boston: Allyn & Bacon.

Tierney, R. J., & Readence, J. E. (2000). *Reading strategies and practices: A compendium* (5th ed.). Boston: Allyn & Bacon.

Tompkins, G. E. (2005). *Language arts: Patterns of practice* (6th ed.). Upper Saddle River, NJ: Merrill/Prentice Hall.

Tompkins, G. E. (2006). *Literacy for the 21st century: A balanced approach* (4th ed.). Upper Saddle River, NJ: Merrill/Prentice Hall.

Vacca, J. A. L., Vacca, R. T., & Gove, M. K. (2000). *Reading and learning to read* (4th ed.). New York: Addison Wesley Longman.

Vacca, R. T., & Vacca, J. A. L. (2005). *Content area reading: Literacy and learning across the curriculum* (8th ed.) Boston: Allyn & Bacon.

Wood, K. D., & Dickinson, T. S. (Eds.). (2000). *Promoting literacy in grades 4–9: A handbook for teachers and administrators.* Boston: Allyn & Bacon.

Children's Literature and Textbook References

Allard, Harry, and James Marshall. *Miss Nelson Has a Field Day*. Houghton Mifflin, 1985.

Allen, Pamela. *Who Sank the Boat?* Coward-McCann, 1982.

Avi. *Crispin: The Cross of Lead*. New York: Hyperion, 2002.

Baron, Harold, Solomon C. Steinfeld, and Robert A. Schultheis. *Practical Record Keeping and Bookkeeping*. South-Western Thompson Learning, 1988.

Bass, Herbert J. *Our Country*: *People in Time and Place*. Silver Burdett Ginn, 1993.

Bender, Lionel. *Lizards and Dragons*. Children's Press, 1991.

Bernstein, Vivian. *American Government*: *Freedom, Rights, Responsibilities*. Steck-Vaughn, 1996.

Bolt, Robert. *A Man For All Seasons*. Random House, 1962.

Brenner, Martha. *Abe Lincoln's Hat*. Illustrated by Donald Cook. Random House, 1994.

Brown, Marc. *Arthur's Teacher Trouble*. Brown, 1994.

Brown, Margaret Wise. *Goodnight Moon*. 1947. Illustrated by Clement Hurd. Harper/Trophy, 1975.

Buffett, Jimmy, and Savannah Jane Buffett. *The Jolly Mon*. Illustrated by Lambert Davis. Harcourt, 1988.

Chapman, Cheryl. *Pass the Fritters, Critters*. Illustrated by Susan L. Roth. Four Winds, 1993.

Cherry, Lynne. *A River Ran Wild*. Harcourt, 1992.

Christopher, Matt. *The Dog that Called the Signals*. Illustrated by Bill Ogden. Brown, 1982.

Climo, Shirley. *The Egyptian Cinderella*. Illustrated by Ruth Heller. HarperCollins, 1989.

Cooney, Timothy and others. *Scott Foresman Science*. Addison-Wesley Educational Publishers, 2000.

Cooper, Elizabeth K. and others. *HBJ Science*. Harcourt Brace Jovanovich, 1989.

Dahl, Roald. *Charlie and the Chocolate Factory*. Knopf, 1964.

Emberly, Barbara. *Drummer Hoff*. Illustrated by Ed Emberly. Simon & Schuster, 1967.

Frankel, Alona. *Prudence's Book of Food*. HarperCollins, 2000.

Gág, Wanda. *The ABC Bunny*. 1933. Coward-McCann, 1992.

Gardiner, John Reynolds. *Stone Fox*. Crowell, 1980.

Garraty, John A. *The Story of America*. Holt, 1991.

George, Jean Craighead. *How to Talk to Your Dog*. HarperCollins, 2000.

Giff, Patricia Reilly. *Next Year I'll Be Special*. Illustrated by Marylin Hafner. Dutton, 1980.

Glubok, Shirley. *The Art of Ancient Egypt Under the Pharaohs*. Atheneum, 1968.

Goble, Paul. *The Girl Who Loved Wild Horses*. Bradbury, 1978.

Golenbock, Peter. *Teammates*. Illustrated by Paul Bacon. Harcourt, 1990.

Guarino, Deborah. *Is Your Mama a Llama?* Illustrated by Steven Kellogg. Scholastic, 1989.

Hopkins, Lee Bennett, ed. *Ring Out Wild Bells*: *Poems about Holidays and Seasons*. Illustrated by Karen Baumann. Harcourt, 1992.

Horne, Paul, Jr. *South Carolina: Its History and Geography*. Atlanta & Clairmont, 2006.

Hubbard, Guy. *Art in Action*. Harcourt, 1996.

Hutchins, Pat. *Rosie's Walk*. Macmillan, 1968.

Jackson, Ellen. *Cinder Edna*. Illustrated by Kevin O'Malley. Lothrop, Lee, & Shepard, 1994.

Jacobs, Joseph. *English Fairy Tales, 1898*. Illustrated by John D. Batten. Dover, 1967.

Keats, Ezra Jack. *Peter's Chair*. Harper, 1967.

Keats, Ezra Jack. *Pet Show!* 1972. Aladdin, 1987.

Kent, Jack. *The Blah*. Parents Magazine, 1970.

Lasky, Kathryn. *The Librarian Who Measured the Earth*. Little, Brown, 1994.

Lauber, Patricia. *The News about Dinosaurs*. Simon & Schuster, 1989.

Leaf, Munro. *The Story of Ferdinand*. Illustrated by Robert Lawson. Viking, 1936.

Leodhas, Sorche Nic. *Gaelic Ghosts*. Illustrated by Nonny Hogrogian. Holt, 1964.

Lionni, Leo. *Fish Is Fish*. Pantheon, 1970.

Lloyd, Alan, et al. *Gregg Keyboarding and Personal Applications*. McGraw-Hill, 1987.

Martin, Rafe. *The Rough-Face Girl*. Illustrated by David Shannon. Putnam's, 1992.

Mayer, Mercer. *Just Me and My Dad*. Golden Books, 1995.

Numeroff, Laura. *If You Give a Mouse a Cookie*. Illustrated by Felicia Bond. Harper, 1985.

Palanti, Margerie. *Piggie Pie*. Illustrated by Howard Fine. Clarion, 1998.

Parish, Peggy. *Dinosaur Time*. Illustrated by Arnold Lobel. HarperCollins, 1974.

Parish, Peggy. *Play Ball, Amelia Bedelia*. Harper & Row, 1972.

Parks, Rosa. *I Am Rosa Parks*. Dial Books for Young Readers, 1997.

Perdomo, Willie. *Visiting Langston*. Illustrated by Bryan Collier. Holt, 2002.

Pfister, Marcus. *The Rainbow Fish*. Translated by J. Alson James. North-South Books, 1992.

Polacco, Patricia. *Pink and Say*. Philomel, 1994.

Prelutsky, Jack, ed. "The Man in the Moon As He Sails the Sky." *Poems of A. Nonny Mouse*. Illustrated by Henrik Drescher. Knopf, 1989.

The Real Mother Goose. Illustrated by Blanche Fisher Wright. Cartwheel Books/Scholastic, 1916.

Reiser, Lynn. *Tortillas and Lullabies/Tortillas y cancioncitas*. Illustrated by Corazones Valientes. Greenwillow, 1998.

Rosenberg, Liz. *Monster Mama*. Illustrated by Stephen Gammell. Putnam, 1993.

Rowan, James P. *I Can Be a Zookeeper*. Children's Press, 1985.

Rylant, Cynthia. *When I Was Young in the Mountains*. Dutton, 1982.

Schmitt, Conrad, and Protase W. Woodford. *Communicating in Spanish*. McGraw-Hill, 1991.

Seuss, Dr. *My Many Colored Days*. Illustrated by Steve Johnson and Lou Fancher. Knopf, 1996.

Sheldon, Dyan. *The Whales' Song*. Illustrated by Gary Blythe. Dial Books for Young Readers, 1991.

Slier, Debby, ed. *The Real Mother Goose Book of American Rhymes*. Illustrated by Patty McCloskey-Padgett, Bernice Loewenstein, and Nan Pollard. Scholastic, 1993.

Sutherland, Zena, and Myra Cohn Livingston, eds. *The Scott, Foresman Anthology of Children's Literature*. Scott, Foresman, 1984.

Swanson, Susan Marie. *The House in the Night*. Illustrated by Beth Krommes. Houghton Mifflin, 2008.

Thayer, Jane. *The Puppy Who Wanted a Boy*. Morrow, 1985.

Waddell, Martin. *Farmer Duck*. Illustrated by Helen Oxenbury. Candewick Press, 1992.

Watkins, Patricia A., and Glenn K. Leto. *Holt Life Science*. Holt, 1994.

Wiesner, David. *Free Fall*. Lothrop, 1988.

Wiesner, David. *Sector 7*. Clarion Books, 1999.

Winter, Jeanette. *Follow the Drinking Gourd*. Knopf, 1988.

Wolfson, Evelyn. *From Abenaki to Zuni: A Dictionary of Native American Tribes*. Illustrated by William Sauts Bock. Walker, 1988.

Yolan, Jane. *Owl Moon*. Illustrated by John Schoenherr. Philomel, 1987.

Yolan, Jane, ed. *Jane Yolan's Mother Goose Songbook*. Musical Arrangements by Adam Stemple. Illustrated by Rosekrans Hoffman. Caroline House. 1992.

Young, Ed. *Lon Po Po: A Red-Riding Hood Story from China*. Penguin/Putnam, 1989.